First World War
and Army of Occupation
War Diary
France, Belgium and Germany

14 DIVISION
Divisional Troops
Machine Gun Corps
14 Battalion
14 June 1918 - 28 February 1919

WO95/1890/2

The Naval & Military Press Ltd
www.nmarchive.com
Published in association with The National Archives

Published by

The Naval & Military Press Ltd

Unit 10 Ridgewood Industrial Park,

Uckfield, East Sussex,

TN22 5QE England

Tel: +44 (0) 1825 749494

www.naval-military-press.com

www.nmarchive.com

This diary has been reprinted in facsimile from the original. Any imperfections are inevitably reproduced and the quality may fall short of modern type and cartographic standards.

© **Crown Copyright**

Images reproduced by permission of The National Archives, London, England, 2015.

Contents

Document type	Place/Title	Date From	Date To
Heading	WO95/1890/2		
Heading	14th Division 14th Bn Machine Gun Corps 1918 Jun-1919 Feb		
War Diary	Grantham	14/06/1918	14/06/1918
Miscellaneous	To:- D.A.G., 3rd Echelon, G.H.Q.	31/07/1918	31/07/1918
War Diary	Grantham	15/06/1918	02/07/1918
War Diary	En Route	03/07/1918	07/07/1918
War Diary	La Maloterie	08/07/1918	13/07/1918
War Diary	Zouafques	14/07/1918	31/07/1918
Miscellaneous			
Miscellaneous	Movement Orders By Lieutenant-Colonel E.R. Meade-Waldo D.S.O. Commanding 14th Battalion, Machine Gun Corps.	11/07/1918	11/07/1918
War Diary	Zouafques	01/08/1918	24/08/1918
War Diary	Proven	26/08/1918	28/08/1918
War Diary	Night Of	28/08/1918	30/08/1918
Miscellaneous	Transport Movement Orders	21/08/1918	21/08/1918
Miscellaneous	March Table To Accompany M.G. 32/2		
Miscellaneous	Movement Orders.		
Miscellaneous	March Table To Accompany M.G. 32/3		
Miscellaneous	14 Battalion M.G. Corps Movement Orders Appendix 5	26/08/1918	26/08/1918
Miscellaneous	Relief Table Issued With M.G. S/40		
Miscellaneous	March Table To Accompany M.G. S. 3/40		
Miscellaneous	No. 14 Machine Gun Battn.	27/08/1918	27/08/1918
War Diary	Ypres Sector Border Camp	31/08/1918	20/09/1918
War Diary	Napier Cotts	20/09/1918	29/09/1918
Operation(al) Order(s)	14 Battalion Machine Gun Corps Order No. 6	01/09/1918	01/09/1918
Operation(al) Order(s)	14 Battalion, Machine Gun Corps Order No. 7	02/09/1918	02/09/1918
Operation(al) Order(s)	14 Battalion Machine Gun Corps Order No. 8	08/09/1918	08/09/1918
Operation(al) Order(s)	14 Battalion Machine Gun Corps Order No. 9	09/09/1918	09/09/1918
Operation(al) Order(s)	No. 14 Machine Gun Battalion Order No. 11	19/09/1918	19/09/1918
Miscellaneous	March Table To Accompany Order No. 11		
Miscellaneous	Train Table To Accompany Order No. 11		
Miscellaneous	Transport Table To Accompany Order No. 11		
Operation(al) Order(s)	No. 14 Machine Gun Battalion Order no. 12	20/09/1918	20/09/1918
Miscellaneous	Amendment To 14 Machine Gun Battalion Order No. 12	20/09/1918	20/09/1918
Miscellaneous	Amendment No. 2 To 14 Machine Gun Battalion Order No. 12	21/09/1918	21/09/1918
Operation(al) Order(s)	14th Battn Machine Gun Corps Order No. 13	25/09/1918	25/09/1918
Miscellaneous	14th Machine Gun Battalion Instructions No. 1	25/09/1918	25/09/1918
Miscellaneous	Fire Organization Orders		
Operation(al) Order(s)	14 M.G. Battn Operation Order No. 20	17/10/1918	17/10/1918
Operation(al) Order(s)	14th Machine Gun Battalion Order No. 21	27/10/1918	27/10/1918
War Diary	Napier Cotts	01/10/1918	02/10/1918
War Diary	Neuve Eglise	03/10/1918	16/10/1918
War Diary	Vauxhall Farm	17/10/1918	17/10/1918
War Diary	Roncq	18/10/1918	19/10/1918
War Diary	Mouscron	20/10/1918	22/10/1918
War Diary	Luingne	23/10/1918	31/10/1918

Type	Description	Date From	Date To
Operation(al) Order(s)	Machine Gun Battalion Order No. 14	01/10/1918	01/10/1918
Miscellaneous	March Table To Accompany M.G. Battalion Order No. 14		
Operation(al) Order(s)	14th Battalion M.G. Corps Operation Order No. 15	05/10/1918	05/10/1918
Operation(al) Order(s)	No. 14 Battn Machine Gun Corps Order No. 16	09/10/1918	09/10/1918
Operation(al) Order(s)	14th Battn Machine Gun Corps Order No. 17	13/10/1918	13/10/1918
Miscellaneous	14th Battn Machine Gun Corps	13/10/1918	13/10/1918
Operation(al) Order(s)	14th Battn Machine Gun Corps Order No. 18	14/10/1918	14/10/1918
Operation(al) Order(s)	14 M G Battn Operation Order No. 19	16/10/1918	16/10/1918
War Diary	Luingne	01/11/1918	02/11/1918
War Diary	Herseaux	03/11/1918	14/11/1918
War Diary	Tourcoing	16/11/1918	30/11/1918
Miscellaneous	14th Machine Gun Batt'n		
Miscellaneous	14th Machine Gun Batt'n	05/11/1918	05/11/1918
Miscellaneous	14th Batt'n, M.G. Corps	05/11/1918	05/11/1918
Operation(al) Order(s)	14th Battn Machine Gun Corps Order No. 23	05/11/1918	05/11/1918
Operation(al) Order(s)	14th Battn Machine Gun Corps Order No. 24	06/11/1918	06/11/1918
Miscellaneous	To:- Officer Commanding,	08/11/1918	08/11/1918
Miscellaneous	Distinguished Conduct Medal		
Operation(al) Order(s)	14th Batt'n, Machine Gun Corps Order No. 25		
Miscellaneous	March Table To Accompany Order No. 25		
War Diary	Tourcoing	30/11/1918	28/02/1919

MS 05/1890(2)

MS 05/1890(2)

14TH DIVISION

14TH BN MACHINE GUN CORPS

~~JLY 1917 – FEB 1919~~

1918 JUN — 1919 FEB

WAR DIARY or INTELLIGENCE SUMMARY.

(Erase heading not required.)

Army Form C. 2118

14 Bn M.G Corps
June & July /18

Instructions regarding War Diaries and Intelligence Summaries are contained in F.S. Regs., Part II. and the Staff Manual respectively. Title pages will be prepared in manuscript.

Place	Date	Hour	Summary of Events and Information	Remarks and references to Appendices
Grantham	14.6.18.		No. 14 Battalion, Machine Gun Corps was formed.	
			Battalion Headquarters.	
			Officer Commanding. Lieut-Colonel E.R.Meade-Waldo D.S.O.	
			Second in Command. Major G.F.Plowden MC.	
			Adjutant. Captain W.F.Lennox.	
			Medical Officer. Captain A. St. Johnston (R.A.M.C.)	
			Quartermaster. Captain F. Tadd.	
			Regimental Sergt.Major. 158925 R.S.M. Dunham R.S.	
			"A" Company.	
			Commanding Company. Major C.G. Stephens MC.	
			Second in Command. Captain D.G. Gayley.	
			Section Officers. Sub-Section Officers.	
			Lieut. E.W.Iredale. 2/Lieut. A. Rees.	
			" W.G.Leggat. " J.C.Lancaster MC	
			" A.W.Murray. " N.Hodgson.	
			" B.J.Phillips. " A.Pool.	
			Transport:- Lieut. C.C. Orrett.	
			"B" Company.	
			Commanding Company. Capt. J.E. Adamson DSO.	
			Second in Command. Lieut. S.H. Merifield.	
			Section Officers. Sub-Section Officers.	
			Lieut. F.K. Ryder. 2/Lieut. J. Herd.	
			2/Lt. E.H. Wale. " G.R. Macdonald.	
			Lieut. W.H. Tunmer. " E.L. Wood.	
			" W.F. Griffin. " H.W. Smart.	
			Transport:- Lieut. W.A. Yearwood.	
			"C" Company.	
			Commanding Company. Capt. D. Baxter MC.	
			Second in Command. Lieut. E.H. Soar MC.	
			Section Officers. Sub-Section Officers.	
			2/Lieut. J.A. Brownley. 2/Lieut. H.G. Gibbs.	
			Lieut. G.H. Acton. " E.T. Lomas.	
			" R.N. Goodeve. Lieut. A.G. Stanbury.	
			D.B./&Le W.Adams/E.M.N. Lees.	
			Transport:- Lieut. C.H. Mansfield.	
			"D" Company.	
			Commanding Company. Capt. C.R. Jackson.	
			Second in Command. Capt. R. Jeffreys.	
			Section Officers. Sub-Section Officers.	
			Lieut. P. Alderson. 2/Lieut. U. Brighton.	
			" A.V.L. Hadaway. " L.L. Moore.	
			" A.S. Davidson. " O.H. Evans.	
			2/Lieut. W.H. Cain. " R. Tasker.	
			Transport:- Lieut. W.B. Baber.	

Ref. No. C.14/

To:- D.A.G.,
    3rd Echelon,
      G. H. Q.

    I send herewith War Diary for the month of July for this Battalion.

In the Field.
31.7.1918.
S.

Lieut-Col.,
Commanding,
No. 14 Machine Gun Battalion.

Army Form C. 2118.

WAR DIARY
or
INTELLIGENCE SUMMARY.
(Erase heading not required.)

Instructions regarding War Diaries and Intelligence Summaries are contained in F. S. Regs., Part II. and the Staff Manual respectively. Title pages will be prepared in manuscript.

Place	Date	Hour	Summary of Events and Information	Remarks and references to Appendices
			Strength of Battn. Officers 49. Other Ranks 879. Horses 237. Vehicles 64.	
			The Other Ranks comprised in addition to the Category "B" men of Battalion Headquarters 35% Category "B" Machine Gunners.	
Grantham.	15.6.1918 to 2.7.1918.		Battalion in process of formation.	
En Route.	3.7.1918.		Transport left Grantham and proceeded via Southampton and HAVRE to join the B.E.F.	
En Route.	5.7.1918.		Remaining Personnel left Grantham and proceeded via FOLKESTONE and BOULOGNE to join the B.E.F.	
			The 14th Battalion being the first complete Machine Gun Battalion to leave ENGLAND.	
En Route.	6.7.1918.		Accommodated at OSTROHOVE Rest Camp.	
	7.7.1918		Proceeded by rail and road to LA MALOTERIE (Map Ref. CALAIS 13) and joined the 14th Division.	
LA MALOTERIE	8.7.1918 to 11.7.1918.		Training.	
	12.7.1918.		Proceeded by road to ALEMBON (Map Ref. CALAIS 13.)	No. 1.
	13.7.1918.		Proceeded by road to ZOUAFQUES (Map Ref. HAZEBROUCK 5a.)	No. 2.
ZOUAFQUES.	14.7.1918 to 16.7.1918.		Training.	
	17.7.1918.		Inspection by General Sir Herbert C.O.PLUMER G.C.N., G.C.M.G., G.C.V.O., A.D.C., Commanding Second Army.	
ZOUAFQUES	17.7.1918 to 31.7.1918.		Training.	

Ref. No.	Date.	Unit.	Starting Point.	Time.	Route	Remarks.
2.	13.7.18.	Battn. H.Q.	Cross Roads immediately East of S. in SANGHEN.	H.Q. 11 a.m.	SANGHEN-LICQUES CLERQUES-HAMEL- GUEMY - ZOUAFQUES.	
"	"	"C" Coy.	"	11-13 am.	"	
"	"	"D" Coy.	"	11-18 am.	"	
"	"	"B" Coy.	"	11-23 am.	"	
"	"	"A" Coy.	"	11-28 am.	"	

SECRET. W.D.

Ref. No.14/S.1/6.

MOVEMENT ORDERS

By

LIEUTENANT-COLONEL E.R.HEALE-WALDO D.S.O.
COMMANDING 14th BATTALION, MACHINE GUN CORPS.

Ref, Calais 15.
Thursday 11th July 1918.

1. **MOVE.** The Battalion will move by road from LA MALOTERIE to ALEMBON on 12th July, 1918.

2. **ROUTE.** The route will be HOULLEFORT, MESNIL, BOURSIN, to ALEMBON.

3. **STARTING POINT.** Cross roads 400^x S. of LA MALOTERIE at top of Corkscrew Bend.

4. **ORDER OF MARCH.** Headquarters, "C" Company, "A" Company, "B" Company, "D" Company. 200 yards distance will be maintained between Companies on the march.

5. **TIMES OF PASSING STARTING POINT.** Head of Companies will pass Starting Point at the following times:-

Headquarters	10-10 a.m.
"C" Company.	10-15 a.m.
"A" Company.	10-18 a.m.
"B" Company.	10-25 a.m.
"D" Company.	10-28 a.m.

6. **RATE OF MARCHING.** 2 miles per hour.

7. **HALTS.** Companies will march and halt as follows.

A	March for 20 minutes from the Clock hour.
B	Halt 10 minutes.
C	March for 20 minutes.
D	Halt 10 minutes and resume march at Clock hour.
E	Halt from 12-30 p.m. to 2-0 p.m. for dinner.

8. **REAR GUARD.** will be furnished by "D" Company. Strength 1 Section Distance 440 yards. Battalion Police will accompany Rear Guard.

[signature]
Captain,
Adjutant, No. 14 M.G. Battalion.

In the Field.
11.7.1918.

Issued to:-
Div. H.Q. A. & Q.	2.
15 Loyal North Lancs. (Pioneers)	1.
S.S.O.	1.
14th Div. Train.	1.
"A" Company.	1.
"B" Company.	1.
"C" Company.	1.
"D" Company.	1.
Battn. Transport Officer.	1.
Battalion Headquarters.	2.
War Diary.	1.
File.	1.

Army Form C. 2118.

14 Bn M.G.Corps

WAR DIARY
or
INTELLIGENCE SUMMARY.

(Erase heading not required.)

Instructions regarding War Diaries and Intelligence Summaries are contained in F. S. Regs., Part II. and the Staff Manual respectively. Title pages will be prepared in manuscript.

Place	Date	Hour	Summary of Events and Information	Remarks and references to Appendices
1918. August 1st to 21st. ZOUAFQUES.			Advanced Training.	
"	14th.		Major J.E.Adamson D.S.O. evacuated (accident with horse). Captain D.C.Cayley assumed Command of "B" Company.	
	22nd.		Battalion prepared to move to PROVEN AREA.	
	22nd.		Battalion transport commenced road march to LEDERZEELE AREA.	See 3.
	22nd.		Battalion marched to NORTHKERQUE in preparation for entraining.	See 4.
	23rd.		Battalion Transport marched to WORMHOUDT. Battalion entrained at NORTHKERQUE and detrained at PROVEN with Battalion Headquarters at MEIGHAN CAMP.	
	24th.		Battalion Transport arrived PROVEN.	
PROVEN.	26th.		Major C.R.Jackson, Officer Commanding "D" Company, and Lieut. W.B.Baber, Transport Officer "D" Company admitted to C.C.S.	
	27th.		Battalion moved to the DIRTY BUCKET AREA in preparation to relieve the 34th Machine Gun Battalion in the line on YPRES Front.	See 5.
	28th.		"B" Coy. relieved 1 Company, 34th Battalion in support. Coy. Headquarters 28.N.W/B.26.5.5. "D" Coy. relieved 1 Coy. 34th Battalion in reserve. 28 N.W. 30. Central.	
Night of 28/29.			"C" Company relieved 1 Coy. 34th Battalion in Front Line Right Sub-Sector, 28.N.W./I.14.b.1.9.	
			(Continued.)	

WAR DIARY
or
INTELLIGENCE SUMMARY.

(Erase heading not required.)

Army Form C. 2118.

Place	Date	Hour	Summary of Events and Information	Remarks and references to Appendices
Night of	August 29/30.		-2-	
	30th		"A" Company relieved 1 Company 54th Battalion in Front Line Left Sub-sector.	
			At conclusion of relief Battalion was situated as follows :-	
			Battalion Headquarters. BORDER CAMP. 28.N.W/A.30.b.3.7.	
			"A" Company. Right Sub-sector. YPRES RAMPARTS,	
			"C" Company. Left " YPRES RAMPARTS.	
			"B" Company. Support. B. 26.c.5.5.	
			"D" Company. Reserve BORDER CAMP. A.30.b.3.7.	
	30.8.1918. S.			

[signature]
Major,
for Commanding,
No. 14 Machine Gun Battalion.

Reference M.G.32/2.

TRANSPORT MOVEMENT ORDERS.

Copy No. _____

Ref.
Sheet 27 1/40,000.
Sheet ST.OMER Combined 1/40,000.   21st August 1918.

(1)   The Battalion Transport under the Command of the Battalion Transport Officer will move to the ST.JANTER BIEZEN Area by March Route staging the night of the
        22nd   LEDERZEELE Area.
        23rd   WORMHOUDT 'C' Area.
March Table for the 22nd inst attached.

(2)   The strictest march discipline will be kept by Units.
The following minimum distances will be maintained -
    (a) Between Transport of Units   100 Yards.
    (b) Between each section of 12 vehicles 50 Yards.

(3)   During the night every precaution will be taken to prevent lights in bivouacs.
The stable guard in addition to their usual duties will report the approach of hostile aircraft by three blasts on the whistle.

(4)   O.C. S.A.A.Section, D.A.C. will arrange to send forward one Officer and two Orderlies for the billeting of the group.
Units will be informed prior to reaching the billetting area the exact location of their billets and the nearest water point.

(5)   The Battalion Transport Officer will detail one Orderly, who will report to the H.Qs., D.A.C. on arrival and will act as runner, He will remain with the D.A.C.H.Qs.

(6)   All further Orders will be issued by the Battalion Transport Officer.

                      (Signed.) W.F.LENNOX, Captain,
                      Adjutant, No. 14 Machine Gun Battalion.

Copies to:-   1 Battalion Transport Officer.
                1 Quartermaster.
                1 "A" Company.
                1 "B" Company.
                1 "C" Company.
                1 "D" Company.
                1 File.
                2 War Diary.

MARCH TABLE TO ACCOMPANY M.G.32/2.

Company.	Starting Point.	Time.	Route.	Remarks.
Headquarters.	Y.M.C.A.	10-15 a.m.	NORDAUSQUES -	(1) Brigade Starting Point Cross Roads NORDAUSQUES.J.21.c.6.1.Time 10-35 a.m.
"A" Company.	"	10-18 a.m.	WESTROVE - GANSPETTE	(2) Head of Battalion Transport not to pass the Cross Roads at J.20.b.5.2. until the 62nd Field Company Transport has passed.
"B" Company.	"	10-21 a.m.	WATTEN - LE BERSTACKE -	(3) Halts will be 10 minutes to the clock hour to the clock hour.
"C" Company.	"	10-24 a.m.	LEDERZEELE	
"D" Company.	"	10-27 a.m.	AREA.	

SECRET.

Appendix. 4

MOVEMENT ORDERS.   M.G. 32/3.

Reference HAZEBROUCK 5A.

(1) **MOVE.**

(a) The Battalion will move to the PROVEN Area by rail on the 23rd entraining at LE VIADUC.
(b) The Battalion will march to the Entraining Station in accordance with March Table attached.

(2) **ENTRAINMENT.**

(a) Transport and Baggage will be prepared to entrain at 4-45 a.m. 23rd. Train departs. 7-45 a.m.
(b) Remainder of Battalion will entrain at 8-45 a.m. 23rd. Train departs 9-45 a.m.

(3) **ACCOMMODATION.**

     MEIGHAN CAMP F.13.a.2.5.
     MONCRIEFF CAMP F.7.c.8.0.
     McCONNELL CAMP F.7.d.2.1.

Hutments will be allotted to Companies on arrival.

(4) **RATIONS.**

(a) Rations for the 23rd will be carried.
(b) Watercarts and Waterbottles will be filled before entrainment.

         (Signed.) W.F.LENNOX, Captain,
      Adjutant, No. 14 Machine Gun Battalion.

Copies to :-

  1 42nd Brigade.
  1 2nd in Command.
  1 Medical Officer.
  1 Quartermaster.
  1 Signalling Officer.
  1 "A" Company.
  1 "B" Company.
  1 "C" Company.
  1 "D" Company.
  1 File.
  1 War Diary.

MARCH TABLE TO ACCOMPANY M.G. 32/3.

Company.	Starting Point.	Time.	Route.	Remarks.
Headquarters.	Y.M.C.A.	22.8.18 6-0 p.m.	LA RECOUSSE -	(1) HALTS.
"A" Company.	"	" 6-2 p.m.	RECQUES -	6-20 p.m. to 6-30 p.m.
"B" Company.	"	" 6-4 p.m.	ZUTKERQUE -	6-50 p.m. to 7-0 p.m.
"C" Company.	"	" 6-6 p.m.	AUDRUICQ -	7-50 p.m. to 8-0 p.m.
"D" Company.	"	" 6-8 p.m.	STEEN STRAATE -	8-50 p.m. to 9-0 p.m.
Transport.	"	" 6-10 p.m.	LE VIADUC.	(2) 100x distance will be maintained between Companies and between "D" Company and Transport.

Appendix 5

SECRET.   M.G.S./40.

14 BATTALION M.G. CORPS MOVEMENT ORDERS

Reference Maps Sheets 27 & 28, 1/40,000.

(1) The Battalion will relieve the 34th Machine Gun Battalion in the Left Divisional Sector of the II Corps Front in accordance with the attached Relief Table.

(2) All details of reliefs will be arranged between Company Commanders concerned.

(3) All Secret Maps, Defence Schemes, Aerial Photos, Schemes of work, Trench Stores, Range Cards, etc, etc., will be taken over.

(4) Completion of all reliefs and moves will be reported to the Battalion Headquarters.

(5) The Battalion will move for the DIRTY BUCKET Area 27th in accordance with the attached March Table.

(Signed.) W.F. LENNOX; Captain,
Adjutant, No. 14 Machine Gun Battalion.

26/8/18

Copies to:-
    14th Div. "Q".   O.C. "A" Coy.
    14th Div. "G".   O.C. "B" Coy.
    41st Inf.Bde.   O.C. "C" Coy.
    42nd Inf.Bde.   O.C. "D" Coy.
    43rd Inf.Bde.   Quartermaster.
    14th Div.Train.   Battalion Transport Officer.
    S.A.A.Sec. D.A.C. 14th Div.
    War Diary.   Signalling Officer.
    File.   Medical Officer.

SECRET.   RELIEF TABLE ISSUED WITH M.G. S/40.

Sheets 27 & 28. 1/40,000.

Serial No.	Date.	Unit.	From.	To.	Unit relieved.	Remarks.
1.	Aug.1918. 27th.	14 M.G.Bn.	PROVEN.	DIRTY BUCKET CAMP.	---------	By March Route.
2.	28th.	"B" Coy.	DIRTY BUCKET CAMP.	Support Position.	1 Coy. 54th M.G.) Battalion.)	Relief to be completed by 6 p.m. 28th August, 1918.
3.	28th.	"D" Coy.	"	Reserve Position.	do.	)
4.	28/29.	"C" Coy.	"	Line Right Bde Sub-Sector	do.	Relief to be completed by 3 a.m. 29th Aug.1918.
5.	29/30.	"A" Coy.	"	Line Left Bde Sub-Sector	do.	Relief to be completed by 3 a.m. 30th Aug.1918.

NOTE:- All movements E. of the GREEN LINE (Trench System running N. and S. through VLAMERTINGHE) will be by Sections at 100 Yards distance.

S E C R E T.

MARCH TABLE TO ACCOMPANY M.G.S.S./40.

Reference Sheets 27 & 28. 1/40,000.

Company.	Starting Point.	Time.	Route.	Remarks.
Headquarters.	"T" Roads. F.7.d.5.5.	2 p.m.	PROVEN - POP ROAD - SWITCH Road in 27.L.6.c.	(1) DISTANCES. 100x between Companies and Transport. 25 X between each six vehicles. (2) HALTS. After 1st 20 minutes 10 minutes halt. After 2nd 20 minutes 10 minutes halt; then at 10.50 minutes to Clock hour to Clock hour. No halt will be made on the Switch Road.
"A" Company.	"	2-30 p.m.	via SWITCH ROAD to POP - ELVERDINGHE Road along ELVERINGHE Road to X Roads in A.23.a.5.0. - Oosthoek - DIRTY BUCKET Camp at A.30.Central.	
"B" Company.	"	3 p.m.		
"C" Company.	"	3-30 p.m.		
"D" Company.	"	4 p.m.		

SECRET. M.G.S.40/1.

Appendix 5

NO. 14 MACHINE GUN BATTN.

ADMINISTRATIVE INSTRUCTIONS WITH REFERENCE TO M.G.S.40.

(1) **S.A.A. Ammunition Supply.**

(a) Corps S.A.A. and Grenade Reserve   GRAYS DUMP 27/E.6.b.8.8.

     Div.   "   "   "   "   STEENJE 28/A.23.a.

     Right Brigade. "   "   "   ST PIERRE 28/I.14.b.1.9.

     Left Brigade. "   "   "   MENIN 28/I.8.b.6.6.

Ammunition issued from the Divisional Dump will be sent forward by the nightly Ration Train.

(b) The following Dumps will be maintained on rear Lines of Defence.

    BROWN LINE   27/H.5.a.9.6.   27/H.11.b.9.5.
    GREEN LINE.   27/H.2.b.7.1.   27/B.26.a.9.4.
    YELLOW LINE. 27/G.6.a.2.4.   27/A.30.b.3.3.

(2) **SUPPLIES.**

(a) The Locations of supply Railhead and Refilling Points in the Forward Area will be notified later. Until these orders are issued the present arrangements will remain in force.

    Rations for "A" & "C" Companies will be sent forward each night from STEENJE MILL SIDING, A.23.a. by Light Railway: the train leaves at 7-45 p.m., 1 truck is reserved for each Company. The Light Railway Staff deliver to such points on the system as Units may require. Supplies are then transhipped to push trucks and pushed forward by Units to the Front System.

(b) **RESERVE RATIONS** of Companies in the Line are located as follows and will be taken over by Units in whose area they are situated:-

    Left M.G.Company.   I.8.a.9.4. 115 Iron Rations.
    Right M.G.Company.   I.14.b.1.9. 85   "   "

(3) **LIGHT RAILWAYS.**

Maps of the Light Railway System should be taken over.
It is desired that the fullest possible use should be made of the system, for the conveyance of Ammunition Supplies, R.E.Stores, and Personnel.
All demands for accommodation will be made by Battalion Headquarters to Div. Headquarters.

(4) **R.E.DUMPS.**

Main Divisional R.E.Dump is at CULLODEN 28/B.26.d.5.0.
Forward dumps to which R.E.material will be delivered under arrangements to be made by the C.R.E.

            ALABAMA   28/I.3.c.5.2.
            ST. PAUL.   28/I.8.d.1.2.
            MELBOURNE   28/I.9.c.2.8.

Further instructions will be issued later.

(5) WATER SUPPLY.

Water tanks have been placed at various points on the Light Railway System and are filled at dawn and dusk by the Light Railway Authorities.

(a)
SALLYPORT YPRES	I.8.d.o.3.	400 Gallon Tank.
YPRES.	I.8.d.1.1.	400 " "
YPRES.	I.8.d.1.7.	200 " "
SAVILLE ROW.	I.8.b.7.7.	400 " "
MENIN ROAD	I.9.c.1.9.	400 " "
MENIN ROAD	I.1.c.8.4.	400 " "
SIEGE CAMP.	B.27.a.5.6.	Two 400 Gallon Tanks.
ORILLIAN CAMP.	H.2.a.6.8.	Two 400 " "

(b) Water Cart Refilling Points exist at the following places in the Divisional Area.

BRAKE CAMP.	28/A.30. Central.
VLAMERTINGHE	28/H.3.b.0.8.
CORNISH CROSS.	28/A.16.a.2.1.
PESELHOEK.	28/A.15.d.6.3.
BRANDHOEK.	28/G.6.c.9.0.

(c) The following is a list of wells in the Divisional Area:-

Location.	Amount of B.P. required per Water Cart per 10 Gall.	Suitability.	Remarks.
I.8.d.3.3.	-------	Not fit for drinking, Cooking or Ablution.	Damaged by shell fire.
I.8.b.9.2.	1 Measure.	Drinking.	----------
I.9.d.4.7.	3 Measures.	"	----------
I.10.c.1.4. White Chau.	2 Measures.	"	----------
I.8.d.7.4.	1 Measure.	"	----------
I.8.d.4.3. Spring East of SALLYPORT.	2 Measures.	"	Issues from Moat Bank.
I.14.c.75.70.	1½ Measures.	"	----------
I.14.c.70.85.	2 Measures.	"	----------
I.13.a.6.3.	2 Measures.	"	----------
I.3.c.2.5.	Over 5 Measures	Ablution only.	Bad smell.
I.3.d.25.25.	2 Measures.	Drinking.	----------
I.4.a.40.25.	Over 6 Measures.	Ablution only.	----------

(G) ROUTES OF EVACUATION.

(1) From Regimental Aid Posts by hand carriage or wheeled stretcher to Collecting Post. DEAD END.

(2)
    (a) From Collecting Post by car direct to Advanced Dressing Station A.30.Central via ESSEX FARM.
    (b) By car direct to Main Dressing Station.
    (c) Walking and slightly Wounded, by Light Railway from DU. HALLOW via ORILLA to PUGWASH SIDING E.6.b.2. thence by Car to Main Dressing Station.

(H) The 42nd Field Ambulance will collect sick from Companies in the Line, and from Headquarters and Reserve Company at DIRTY BUCKET CORNER.

(10) THEATRE. is situated at A.30. Central where the Divisional Troupe will perform.

(11) MISCELLANEOUS.

Steel Helmets will be worn and Box Respirators carried at the "ALERT" position EAST of the Grid Line (Sheet 28) H.9.a.0 - H.3.a.0.0. - B.21.a.0.0. - B.15.a.0.7.

(12) List of All TRENCH STORES, MAPS, etc taken over will be forwarded to these Headquarters by 12 Noon 30th August, 1918.

                          (Signed.) W.F.LENNOX, Captain,
27.8.1918.   Adjutant, No. 14 Machine Gun Battalion.

Copies to:-
14th Div."G".	42nd Field Ambulance.
14th Div."Q".	O.C. "A" Company.
41st Inf.Bde.	O.C. "B" Company.
42nd Inf.Bde.	O.C. "C" Company.
43rd Inf. Bde.	O.C. "D" Company.
2nd in Command.	Signals.
Battn.Transport Officer.	Quartermaster.
War Diary.	Medical Officer.
File.	

-3-

(6) **BATHS.**

Baths are in operation at the following places:-

SIEGE BATHS	B.20.d.9.1.
SARATOGA BATHS	A.30.a.6.4.
LILLE GATE YPRES	
"P" Camp.	28/A.15.d.3.6.
"X" Camp.	28/A.23.c.3.5.

(7) **CEMETERIES.**

YPRES RESERVOIR NORTH CEMETERY	28/I.7.b.1.4. to be used only in case of emergency.
MENDINGHEM.	27/E.6.d.10.9.5.
HAGLE DUMP.	28/G.6.a.3.7.
NINE ELMS.	27/L.10.b.35.45.

(8) **TRAFFIC.**

During/and subsequent to wet weather, Tracks "A", "B" & "C" will not be used by Transport.

Transport of Units in the Line, which is proceeding EAST of YPRES - COMINES Canal will not pass the line - GOLDFISH Chateau - BRIELEN before 9-15 p.m.

(9) **MEDICAL ARRANGEMENTS** Reference Map Sheets 19, 27 & 28 1/40,000.

(A) **REGIMENTAL AID POSTS.**

(a) Right Brigade.   I.14.b.1.7.
                        H.11.b.2.0.
(b) Left Brigade.   I.9.a.2.9.   SAVILLE ROAD.
                        I.8.d.1.5.   RAMPARTS.
                        I.9.d.0.6.   MENIN ROAD.

(B) **ADVANCED DRESSING STATION.**   28/A.30. Central.

(C) MAIN DRESSING STATION.)
    GAS CENTRE.   )   19/A.23.a.4.9. ROUSEBRUGGE.
    DIVISIONAL REST STATION)

(D) WALKING WOUNDED COLLECTING POST (for active operations).
                                 28/H.1.b.7.1.TAVISTOCK HOUSE.

(E) LOCAL SICK COLLECTING STATION.   27/F.29.b.8.2.
                                                  L'EBBE FARM.

(F) **FIELD AMBULANCE LOCATIONS.**

44th Field Ambulance.   BOLLEZEELE 27/A.22.c & d.
                       1 Section will be at L'EBBE FARM 27/F.29.b.8.2.

43rd Field Ambulance.   ROUSEBRUGGE 19/W.23.a.4.9.

42nd Field Ambulance.   28/A.30. Central.

Army Form C. 2118.

14 Bn M.G. Corps
68 D 4

WAR DIARY
or
INTELLIGENCE SUMMARY.
(Erase heading not required.)

Instructions regarding War Diaries and Intelligence Summaries are contained in F. S. Regs., Part II. and the Staff Manual respectively. Title pages will be prepared in manuscript.

Place	Date	Hour	Summary of Events and Information	Remarks and references to Appendices
YPRES Sector BORDER CAMP.	31st Aug.		Companies settled in position, conditions quiet, one casualty (Head Wound Shrapnel)	
	1st Sept.		Condition normal. No change.	
"	2nd		"D" Company relieved "B" Company in Support.	No. 6.
"	3/4 Sep.		"B" Company relieved "C" Company in CANAL Sector.	No. 7.
"	5th.		Normal. 2/Lieut. W.G.Massey reported and is posted to "B" Company.	
"	6th.		Normal.	
"	7th.		Normal. Major C.R.Jackson & Lieut. W.B.Baber evacuated and struck off strength.	
"	8th.		Normal.	
"	9th.		"C" Company relieved "D" Company in support.	No. 8.
"	9th.		Lieut. A.V.L. Hadaway "D" Company admitted F.A. with fractured ankle and struck off strength 16.9.1918.	
"	10th.		"D" Company relieved "A" Company in Left Brigade Sub-Sector.	No. 9.
"	11th.		Normal.	
"	12th.		Normal. Lieuts W.H.Roberts and O.P.Ladly reported and posted to "D" Company.	
"	13th & 14th.		Conditions Normal.	
"	15th		1 Casualty (Killed in Action G.S.W.)	
"	16th & 17th.		Conditions Normal.	
			(Continued.)	

Army Form C. 2118.

WAR DIARY
or
INTELLIGENCE SUMMARY.
(Erase heading not required.)

Instructions regarding War Diaries and Intelligence Summaries are contained in F. S. Regs., Part II. and the Staff Manual respectively. Title pages will be prepared in manuscript.

Place	Date	Hour	Summary of Events and Information	Remarks and references to Appendices
YPRES Sector. BOESIGHE CAMP.	Sept. 19th/ 20th.		Battalion relieved in YPRES Sector by 9th and 29th Machine Gun Battalions and proceeded to YPRES – COMINES CANAL Sector. Locations, Reference Sheets 27 & 28 1/40,000. Battalion Headquarters G.23.d.9.1. NAPIER COTTAGES.	No. 11.
			"A" Company. L.20.b.5.9. "B" Company. G.19.b.8.8.	
			"C" Company. H.28.a.4.9. "D" Company. G.19.a.5.8.	
NAPIER COTTS.	20th.		Conditions Normal, 1 casualty 2/Lieut. H.G.Gibbs wounded slightly, evacuated.	
"	21st		Conditions normal 1 casualty (1 Other Rank Killed in Action).	
"	Night of 21/22nd.		"A" and "C" Companies take over Gun Positions from 35th Machine Gun Battalion.	No. 12.
"	23rd.		"B" Company, 101st Machine Gun Battalion become attached to No. 14 Machine Gun Battalion.	
"	24th.		Casualties 2 Officers (Lieut. W.P.Griffin and Lieut. W.A.Yearwood(Wounded) 1 Officer, Lieut. D.J.Mowat "B" Company, 101st Machine Gun Battalion (Killed in Action). 10 Other Ranks wounded.	
"	24th.		2/Lieut. J.E.Paton reported from Base Depot, CAMIERS and was posted to "B" Company as Transport Officer vice Lieut. W.A.Yearwood. (Wounded 24.9.1918.)	
"	25th.		Casualties Lieut. C.G.Orrett (Killed in Action) 1 Other Rank (Killed in Action) 3 Other Ranks wounded.	
"	26th.		Normal. Conditions.	
"	27th.		Casualty 1 Other Rank wounded.	
"	28th.		Battalion took part in the attack made by 14th Division in accordance with Operations Orders attached.	No. 13.

Army Form C. 2118.

WAR DIARY
or
INTELLIGENCE SUMMARY.
(Erase heading not required.)

*Instructions regarding War Diaries and Intelligence Summaries are contained in F.S. Regs., Part II. and the Staff Manual respectively. Title pages will be prepared in manuscript.

Place	Date	Hour	Summary of Events and Information	Remarks and references to Appendices
NAPIER GOTTS.	Sept. 28th		(1) The distribution of the 14th Machine Gun Battalion and "B" Company, 101st Machine Gun Battalion attached for the Operations 28th September were as follows :-	
			The Battalion was divided into two Groups, one Group working with each of the two Infantry Brigades carrying out the attack.	
			(a)	
			The composition of the Groups were/with the 42nd Infantry Brigade	
			RIGHT GROUP.	Guns.
			Three Barrage Batteries each of 8 Guns.	24.
			Forward Guns - Two Sections.	8.
			Brigade Reserve - One Section.	4.
			Total.	36.
			(b) With 43rd Infantry Brigade.	
			Three Barrage Batteries each of 8 Guns.	24.
			Forward Guns - Two Sections.	8.
			Battery of Opportunity - One Section.	4.
			Brigade Reserve - One Section.	4.
			Total.	40.
			Divisional Reserve - One Section.	4.
			Grand Total.	44.
			(2) The Barrage Batteries fired a Creeping Barrage to cover the Infantry Advance. This Barrage involved 5 lifts each of 300 Yards.	
			/(Continued.)	

Army Form C. 2118.

WAR DIARY
or
INTELLIGENCE SUMMARY.
(Erase heading not required.)

Place	Date	Hour	Summary of Events and Information	Remarks and references to Appendices
BAPIER COTTS.	Sept. 28th.		(2) Continued.	

The Barrage was fired without a hitch and according to the testimony of the Infantry was most effective, there were no complaints of short shooting. About 250,000 rounds were fired in order to be able to place a S.O.S. Barrage beyond the final objective in the neighbourhood of the WHITE CHATEAU, it was necessary to move forward the Left Battery of the Left Group, this move was carried out promptly by two Sections 101st Machine Gun Battalion.

(3) The Forward Guns on both Brigade Fronts moved forward immediately behind the Infantry Supports, they had no difficulty in getting forward, owing to the poor resistance by the enemy they had very little to do. The Section with the 6th Wilts came into action/with good effect, and one Gun Team appears to have done good work in clearing out Enemy Snipers. They claim to have shot a German Officer and 5 men with their Revolvers.

(4) The Battery of Opportunity with the Left Brigade found great difficulty in getting forward sufficiently quickly to be of value owing to the very heavy going in the neighbourhood of THE BLUFF. The rain and mist and the smoke of the barrage prevented them from seeing sufficiently well to be able to engage any targets. The Battery took up a position in the neighbourhood of BLUFF JUNCTION as part of the Consolidation Scheme, its role being to stop a Counter-attack debouching from the DAMMSTRASSE.

(5) The Section in Divisional Reserve were ready to move with Guns etc., on Mule Pack, they were not called upon.

(6) The following lessons seem to be brought out by the action :-

(a) Batteries of Opportunity are not of much value unless the ground is exceptionally favourable and the attack takes place by day.

(b) That Infantry Battalions must understand that Forward Machine Gun Sections working with them communicate through their Headquarters. Many messages were sent in by Forward Sections to Battalion Headquarters but the latter did not seem to realise the necessity of transmitting them to Brigade Headquarters. In the present case there should have been no difficulty as the telephone lines was maintained within 300 yards of the Battn Headquarters throughout Operations.

Army Form C. 2118.

WAR DIARY
or
INTELLIGENCE SUMMARY.
(Erase heading not required.)

Instructions regarding War Diaries and Intelligence Summaries are contained in F. S. Regs., Part II, and the Staff Manual respectively. Title pages will be prepared in manuscript.

Place	Date	Hour	Summary of Events and Information	Remarks and references to Appendices
NAPIER COTTS.	Sept. 28th.		(6) Continued.	
			(c) Each Company had its establishment of S.A.A. with it consisting of 146,000 rounds per Company, in addition each Group had 150,000 Rounds. This was found to be far in excess of requirements and could be reduced with advantage.	
			(7) The casualties incurred were very slight.	
			Officers. Other Ranks.	
			(a) During preparations. 1. 20.	
			(b) During Operations. - 8.	
			TOTAL. 1. 28.	
"	29th.		Companies withdrawn from the Line and concentrated at NAPIER COTTAGES.	

                  Lieut-Col.,
                  Commanding,
              No. 14 Machine Gun Batt'n.

SECRET.   Copy No. 14

14 BATTALION MACHINE GUN CORPS ORDER NO. 56.

Reference Map Sheet 28 N.W.   1.9.1918.

(1)   The following relief will take place on the 2nd instant :-

   "D" Company will relieve "B" Company in support with Headquarters at B.26.Central.

   "B" Company will retire for the night to BORDER CAMP.

(2)   Relief of the guns in I.13.A. will not take place till after dark.

(3)   All Defence Schemes, Air Photos, Trench Maps, Anti-Gas Appliances, S.A.A, &c., and other trench and area stores will be carefully handed over and receipts obtained.

(4)   All permanent working parties and guards will be carefully taken over by the relieving Company in each case.

(5)   All information regarding the enemy and details of work in hand and proposed will be taken over by Companies on relief.

(6)   All other details of relief will be arranged direct between O.C's concerned.

(7)   Completion of relief will be reported to Battalion Headquarters by telegraph code word "FUSEE".

(8)   Movement E. of VLAMERTINGHE will be by sections at 100 yards distance.

(9)   Acknowledge.

                              (Signed.) W.F.LENNOX, Captain,
                              Adjutant, No. 14 Machine Gun Battalion.

Copies to:-

1. 14th Div."G".
2. 14th Div."Q".
3. 41st Inf.Bde.
4. 42nd Inf.Bde.
5. 43rd Inf.Bde.
6. "A" Company.
7. "B" Company.
8. "C" Company.
9. "D" Company.
10. Quartermaster.
11. Signals.
12. Medical Officer.
13. Battn.Transport Officer.
14.)
15.) War Diary.
16.)
16. File.

SECRET.   Copy No. 14

14 BATTALION, MACHINE GUN CORPS
ORDER NO. 87.

Reference Map Sheet 28 N.W.   2.9.1918.

(1)   The following relief will take place on the night of the 3rd instant :-

    "B" Company will relieve "C" Company in the Right Brigade Sub-Sector with Headquarters at I.14.b.1.9.

    "C" Company will be placed in reserve with Headquarters at BORDER CAMP.

(2)   Relief will be carried out after dark.   "B" Company will not be EAST of the ELVERDINGHE - VLAMERTINGHE ROAD before 8 p.m.

(3)   Movement EAST of VLAMERTINGHE will be by sections at 100 yards distance.

(4)   All Defence Schemes, Air Photos, Trench Maps, Anti-Gas Appliances, S.A.A. &c, and other Trench and area stores will be carefully handed over and receipts obtained.

(5)   All permanent working parties and guards will be carefully taken over by the relieving Company in each case.

(6)   All information regarding the enemy and details of work in hand and proposed will be taken over by Companies on relief.

(7)   All other details of relief will be arranged direct between O's.C Companies concerned.

(8)   Completion of relief will be reported to Battalion Headquarters by telegraph code word "CRANK".

(9)   Acknowledge.

                                        (Signed.) W.F.LENNOX, Captain,
                                Adjutant, No. 14 Machine Gun Battalion.

Copies to :-

     1. 14th Division "G".   8. "C" Company.
     2. 14th Division "Q".   9. "D" Company.
     3. 41st Inf. Bde.   10. Quartermaster.
     4. 42nd Inf. Bde.   11. Signals.
     5. 43rd Inf. Bde.   12. Medical Officer.
     6. "A" Company.   13. Battn. Transport Officer.
     7. "B" Company.   14)
                                     15) War Diary.
                                     16. File.

SECRET.   Copy No. 14

14 BATTALION MACHINE GUN CORPS
ORDER No. 8.

Reference Map Sheet 28 N.W.   8.9.1918.

(1)   The following relief will take place on the 9th instant.

"C" Company will relieve "D" Company in support with Headquarters at B.26.c.5.5.

"D" Company will retire for the night to BORDER CAMP.

(2)   Relief of the guns in I.13.A. will not take place till after dark.

(3)   All Defence Schemes, Air Photos, Trench Maps, Anti-Gas Appliances, S.A.A, &c., and other trench and area stores will be carefully handed over and receipts obtained.

(4)   All permanent working parties and guards will be carefully taken over by the relieving Company in each case.

(5)   All information regarding the enemy and details of work in hand and proposed will be taken over by Companies on relief.

(6)   All other details of relief will be arranged direct between Officers Commanding Companies concerned.

(7)   Completion of relief will be reported to Battalion Headquarters by telegraph code word "SPRING".

(8)   Movement E. of VLAMERTINGHE will be by Sections at 100 yards distance.

(9)   Acknowledge.

                                    (Signed.) W.F.LENNOX, Captain,
                                Adjutant, No. 14 Machine Gun Battalion.

Copies to :-

1. 14th Div. "G".
2. 14th Div. "Q".
3. 41st Inf. Bde.
4. 42nd Inf. Bde.
5. 43rd Inf. Bde.
6. "A" Company.
7. "B" Company.
8. "C" Company.
9. "D" Company.
10. Quartermaster.
11. Signals.
12. Medical Officer.
13. Battn. Transport Officer.
14.) War Diary.
15.)
16. File.

SECRET.   Copy No. 15

14 BATTALION MACHINE GUN CORPS

ORDER NO. 9.

Reference Map Sheet 28 N.W.   9.9.1918.

(1) The following relief will take place on the night of the 10th instant.

"D" Company will relieve "A" Company in the Left Brigade Sub-Sector with Headquarters at I.8.b.00.30.

"A" Company will be placed in reserve with Headquarters at BORDER CAMP.

(2) Relief will be carried out after dark. "D" Company will not be EAST of the ELVERDINGHE - VLAMERTINGHE ROAD before 8 p.m.

(3) Movement EAST of VLAMERTINGHE will be by sections at 100 yards distance.

(4) All Defence Schemes, Air Photos, Trench Maps, Anti-Gas Appliances, S.A.A. &c., and other Trench and area stores will be carefully handed over and receipts obtained.

(5) All permanent working parties and guards will be carefully taken over by the relieving Company in each case.

(6) All information regarding the enemy and details of work in hand and proposed will be taken over by Companies on relief.

(7) All other details of relief will be arranged direct between Officers Commanding Companies concerned.

(8) Completion of relief will be reported to Battalion Headquarters by telegraph, Code word "TRIP".

(9) Acknowledge.

                                        (Signed.) W.F.LENNOX, Captain,
                                   Adjutant, No. 14 Machine Gun Battalion.

Copies to :-

1. 14th Division "G".
2. 14th Division "Q".
3. 41st Inf. Bde.
4. 42nd Inf. Bde.
5. 43rd Inf. Bde.
6. "A" Company.
7. "B" Company.
8. "C" Company.
9. "D" Company.
10. Quartermaster.
11. Signals.
12. Medical Officer.
13. Battn. Transport Officer.
14.)
15.) War Diary.
16. File.

SECRET.   NO. 14 MACHINE GUN BATTALION   Copy No. 16

ORDER No. 11.

(1) On the night of the 19/20th September, the Battalion will be relieved by the 9th and 29th Machine Gun Battalions in the YPRES Sector.

(2) (a) "B" Company will be relieved in the CANAL SECTOR by "C" Company 29th Machine Gun Battalion.

"D" Company will be relieved in the YPRES SECTOR by "A" Company, 9th Machine Gun Battalion.

(b) Relief will be completed by 12 Midnight.

(3) All Maps, schemes, Trench Stores, etc., etc., will be handed over and receipts obtained.

(4) All moves will be carried out in accordance with attached tables.

(5) Completion of reliefs and moves will be reported to this Office.

(6) On completion of move the Battalion will be located as follows :-

    Battalion Headquarters   G.23.d.9.1. (NAPIER COTTAGES)
    "A" Company.   27/L.20.b.5.9.
    "B" Company.   28/G.19.a.5.8.
    "C" Company.   Line (Coy. Headquarters H.28.a.4.9.)
    "D" Company.   28/G.19.a.5.8.
    Quartermaster's Stores.   28/G.19.a.5.8.

(7) Battalion Headquarters will close at BORDER CAMP at 5-30 p.m. and open at G.23.d.9.1. at the same hour.

(8) ACKNOWLEDGE.

(Signed.) W.F. LENNOX, Captain,
Adjutant, No. 14 Machine Gun Battalion.

19.9.1918.

Copies to :-
1. 14th Div. "G".
2. 14th Div. "Q".
3. "A" Coy. 9th M.G.Batt'n.
4. "C" Coy. 29th M.G.Batt'n.
5. 26th Inf. Bde.
6. 41st Inf. Bde.
7. 43rd Inf. Bde.
8. 42nd Inf. Bde.
9. "A" Company.
10. "B" Company.
11. "C" Company.
12. "D" Company.
13. Quartermaster.
14. Medical Officer.
15. Signals.
16.) War Diary.
17.)
18. File.
19. B.T.O.

S E C R E T.

APPENDIX "A".

MARCH TABLE TO ACCOMPANY ORDER NO. 11.

Reference Sheets 27/28 1/40,000.

Company.	Starting Point.	Destination.	Time.	Route.	Remarks.
Batt'n Headquarters.	BORDER CAMP.	G.23.d.9.1.	5-30 p.m.	YORK CROSS - South to X Roads at LINDE GOED Farm - S.E. to X Roads G.24.c. Central - S.W. to G.23.d.9.1.	(1) Usual intervals to be maintained.
"A" Company.	BORDER CAMP.	27/L.20.b.5.9.	5-30 p.m.	ST.JOHN CROSS - POPERINGHE - South to 27/L.17.b.30.20.- S.W. to 27/L.21.c. 4.5. - N.W. to 27/L.20.b.5.9.	

SECRET.

APPENDIX "B".

TRAIN TABLE TO ACCOMPANY ORDER NO. 11.

Reference 27/28 1/40,000.

Company.	Time.	Size of Train.	Entraining Station.	Detraining Station.	Remarks.
"B" Company.	12-30 a.m.	8 Trucks.	MACHINE GUN SIDING.	REMY NORTH 27/L.23.a.6.5.	
"D" Company.	12-30 a.m.	8 Trucks.	MACHINE GUN SIDING.	-do-	

S E C R E T.

TRANSPORT TABLE TO ACCOMPANY ORDER NO. 11.

APPENDIX "C".

Reference Sheets 27 & 28 1/40,000.

Company.	Starting Point.	Destination.	Time.	Route.	Remarks.
Headquarters.	ST. JOHN'S CROSS.	28/G.19.a.5.8.	5-0 p.m.	ST. JOHN'S CROSS - POPERINGHE - South, in 28/G.I.d. down road to 27/L.17.b.20.10.- E.E. to 28/G.19.a.5.8.	(1) Usual intervals to be maintained. (2) Transport of "B" & "D" Companies to move under orders of Company Transport Officers. (3) "C" Company's Transport to proceed to destination under orders to be issued by Officer Commanding "C" Company.
"B" Company.) "D" Company.)	ST. JOHN'S CROSS.	28/G.19.a.5.8.	5-5 p.m. 5-10 p.m.	ditto.	
"A" Company.	With Company.	27/L.20.b.50.90.	5-30 p.m.		
"C" Company.		27/L.20.b.50.90.			

SECRET.   Copy No. 16

NO. 14 MACHINE GUN BATTALION

ORDER NO. 12.

Reference Sheet 28 S.W.

(1) The Machine Gun defence of the Divisional Front will be re-organized on the night 21/22nd September, so as to make one Company responsible for each Brigade Sub-Sector. In order to effect this the following moves and reliefs will take place :-

(2) "A" Company will take over the Machine Gun Defence of the Left Brigade Front.
   The following positions will be taken over :-

   (a) 4 positions in the neighbourhood of LOCK 8 - I.32.a. from "C" Company, 14th Machine Gun Battalion.

   (b) 4 positions EAST of KRUISSTRAATHOEK in I.30.d. from 35th Machine Gun Battalion.

(3) "C" Company will over from support Company, 35th Machine Gun Battalion, two positions at I.30.c.0.5.

   Headquarters of Support Company, 35th Machine Gun Battalion is at AMBULANCE FARM H.14.b.7.4.

(4) All permanent working parties and guards will be carefully taken over by the relieving Company in each case.

(5) All information regarding the enemy and details of work in hand and proposed will be taken over by Companies on relief.

(6) All other details of relief will be arranged direct between Officers Commanding Companies concerned.

(7) Completion of relief will be reported to Battalion Headquarters by telegraph, Code word, "COME".

(8) Companies to acknowledge.

                              (Signed.) W.F. LENNOX, Captain,
                              Adjutant, No. 14 Machine Gun Battalion.
20.9.1918.
S.

Copies to :-

1. 14th Div. "G".
2. 14th Div. "Q".
3. 41st Inf. Bde.
4. 42nd Inf. Bde.
5. 43rd Inf. Bde.
6. 35th Bn. M.G.C.
7. "A" Company.
8. "B" Company.
9. 35th Div. "G".
10. "C" Company.
11. "D" Company.
12. Signals.
13. Medical Officer.
14. B. T. O.
15. Support Coy. 35th Bn. M.G.C.
16.) War Diary.
17.)
18. File.

SECRET.

Amendment to 14 Machine Gun Battalion Order No. 12.

Para. 2 (b) for I.30.d. read H.30.d.
Para. 3 for I.30.c.0.5. read H.30.c.0.5.

(Signed.) W.F.LENNOX, Captain,
Adjutant, No. 14 Machine Gun Batt'n.

20.9.1918.

Issued to all Recipients of Order No. 12.

S E C R E T.

Amendment No. 2 to 14 Machine Gun Battalion Order No. 12.

Para. 2 (a) For "from "C" Company, 14th Machine Gun Battalion " read 35th Machine Gun Battalion.

Para. 2 (b) For "from 35th Machine Gun Battalion" read "C" Company, 14th Machine Gun Battalion.

(Signed.) W.F.LENNOX, Captain,
Adjutant, No. 14 Machine Gun Batt'n.

21.9.1918.

Issued to all Recipients of Order No. 12.

SECRET.   Copy No. 10

14th Battn Machine Gun Corps

ORDER NO. 13.

(1) (a) The 14th Division will carry out an attack on "J" Day in conjunction with the 34th Division on their right and the 35th Division on their left. The 1st and 2nd objectives for the attack and Inter-Divisional and Inter-Brigade Boundaries and the forming up line for the attack are shown on map X issued with Machine Gun Instructions.

(b) The attack S.W. of the YPRES - COMINES Canal will go straight through to the 1st objective - North of the Canal there will be a pause on the line - THE BLUFF inclusive - THE CATERPILLAR inclusive. The advance from this line to the 1st objective line North of the YPRES - COMINES Canal and to the 2nd objective line south of the Canal will be resumed at H + 96 minutes.

(2) (a) The 14th Division is attacking, the 42nd Infantry Brigade on the right and the 43rd Infantry Brigade on the left.

(b) The capture of the ST. ELOI Craters is allotted to the 42nd Infantry Brigade and the capture of THE BLUFF to the 43rd Infantry Brigade, these objectives are to be gained and held at all costs.

(c) The forming up line for the attack is the line - OLD FRENCH TRENCH and MIDDLESEX ROAD within the Divisional Boundaries.

(3) The 41st Infantry Brigade will be in Divisional Reserve.

(4) The attack as far as the 1st objective will be carried out under an Artillery Barrage moving at a pace of 100 yards in 3 minutes, with a first lift 4 minutes after "H". After H + 45 minutes batteries will search backwards and forwards to a depth of 500 yards firing 3 minute bursts. At H + 96 the Artillery Creeping Barrage will come down again in front of the Sector of the 43rd Infantry Brigade and will remain stationary for 4 minutes, lifting off at H + 100 and continuing to lift at the rate of 100 yards in 3 minutes. The Infantry during the advance will move as close to the Artillery Barrage as possible. There will be no regular Barrage in front of the 42nd Infantry Brigade after their 1st objective has been taken, but the Infantry will endeavour to gain ground towards the 2nd objective in co-operation with the 43rd Infantry Brigade.

(5) (a) The action of the 14th Machine Gun Battalion and "B" Company 101st Machine Gun Battalion which is attached for these operations will be as already laid down in Machine Gun Instructions No. 1.

(b) The forward Guns will be detailed from the Companies now in the line

"C" Company for the 42nd Infantry Brigade,
"A" Company for the 43rd Infantry Brigade.

(c) The Battery of Opportunity will be detailed from "A" Company.

(d) The detailing of Reserve Sections is left to Group Commanders but the Companies to which they belong will be notified to Battalion Headquarters.

P.T.O.

(5) Continued:)

(e) "B" Company, 101st Machine Gun Battalion will be withdrawn from the Line on completion of its Barrage Task and will be concentrated as soon as circumstances permit in the neighbourhood of "A" and "C" Company's Headquarters H.22.c.4.1. and come into Divisional Reserve — completion of this move will be reported to Divisional Headquarters. The Transport Animals of this Company will be harnessed ready to move but not hooked in by H + 4 hours.

(6) The Battalion Commander will be attached to Divisional Headquarters HAGUE FARM after "H". Group Commanders can communicate with him there on the Brigade Lines from Advanced Brigade Headquarters. The 2nd in Command and Quartermaster will be at Battalion Headquarters NAPIER COTTS and can be communicated with either through Advanced Divisional Headquarters or through the Company Headquarters in H.22.c.4.1.

All Administrative questions should be addressed to NAPIER COTTS.

A portion of the Transport of all Companies will be kept near NAPIER COTTS for use if required.

(7) Group Commanders will synchronise watches with the Brigades with which they are working. The signal for the opening of the Machine Gun Barrage will be the opening of the Artillery Barrage — no Machine Guns will open fire except on a S.O.S. before the opening of the Artillery Barrage.

(8) Medical and Administrative Instructions will be issued separately.

(9) A C K N O W L E D G E.

25.9.1918.
                                                             Captain,
                                      Adjutant, No. 14 Machine Gun Batt'n.

Copies to:-
1. O.C. Right Group.
2. O.C. Left Group.
3. "A" Company.
4. "B" Company.
5. "C" Company.
6. "D" Company.
7. "B" Coy. 101st M.G.Batt'n.
8. 2nd in Command.
9. Quartermaster.
10.)
11.) War Diary.
12. File.

SECRET.   Copy No. _____

14th MACHINE GUN BATTALION

INSTRUCTIONS NO. 1.

(1) (a)   The Machine Guns at the disposal of the Division will be divided into two Groups and Divisional Reserve.

(b) <u>Right M.G.Group</u> - Commander Major D.Baxter M.C.   To support the 42nd Infantry Brigade.

    <u>Composition</u> -   "B" Company, 14th M.G.Battalion.
                        "C" Company, 14th M.G.Battalion.
                        Two Sections, 101st M.G.Battalion.

   N.B.   One Section to be detailed as Divisional Reserve.

(c) <u>Left M.G.Group.</u> - Commander Major C.G.Stephens M.C.   To support the 43rd Infantry Brigade.

    <u>Composition.</u> -   "A" Company, 14th M.G.Battalion.
                         "D" Company, 14th M.G.Battalion.
                         Two Sections, 101st M.G.Battalion.

(d) Divisional Reserve - One Section to be detailed by Right Group.

(e) In addition the 34th Machine Gun Battalion will co-operate with fire on localities on the front and right flank of the 42nd Infantry Brigade, the areas to be fired on are shown on attached map X.

(2) The distribution of the Machine Guns in the Groups will be as follows:-

<u>RIGHT M.G.GROUP.</u>

   <u>Forward Guns.</u>   Two Sections.

   <u>Rear Guns.</u>   One Company, Two Sections.

   <u>Reserve Guns.</u>   One Section.

<u>LEFT M.G.GROUP.</u>

   <u>Forward Guns.</u>   Two Sections.

   <u>Rear Guns.</u>   One Company, Two Sections.

<u>BATTERY OF OPPORTUNITY.</u>   One Section.

<u>RESERVE.</u>   One Section.

(3) The Sections detailed as Forward Guns will be at the disposal of the B.G.C. 42nd and 43rd Infantry Brigades respectively, detail as to their employment will be arranged by Group Commanders with the Brigadiers concerned.

                                                                                 P.T.O.

-2-

(4) The Rear Guns will fire a Creeping Barrage and Concentrations, details of which are shown on the attached Chart, and Map X.

The Batteries firing North of the YPRES - COMINES Canal and for 300 yards South will not be able to fire on their Barrage Lines during the advance from the Line - THE BLUFF - I.34.d.3.5. to the second objective. They will be prepared to fire a concentration on the area WHITE CHATEAU - The STABLES in O.4.d.

(5) The Battery of Opportunity operating with the 43rd Infantry Brigade will move forward so as to reach points from which good forward observation is obtainable as early as possible after their capture. The object of the Battery is to seize every opportunity of inflicting loss on the enemy - to give close support by direct fire to the infantry during the advance and during counter-attacks, and to engage low-flying Hostile Aeroplanes. It will endeavour to obtain a position on THE BLUFF from which it can support the advance from the line - THE BLUFF - I.34.d.3.5. to the second objective line with direct overhead fire.

(6) The Sections in reserve will be complete with Pack Transport.

(a) The Sections in reserve with Groups are at the disposal of the B.G.C's 42nd and 43rd Infantry Brigades respectively.

(b) The Section in Divisional Reserve will be located at H.22.c.4.1. ("A" and "C" Company's Headquarters) and will not be moved without orders from Divisional Headquarters.

(7) On completion of its task the Company 101st M.G.Battalion will be withdrawn from the line as soon as practicable and will be concentrated in the neighbourhood of the Company Headquarters in H.22.c.4.1. Completion of move to be reported to Divisional Headquarters.

(8) On completion of their Barrage Tasks Left Group Commander will be prepared to move forward Batteries to place an S.O.S.Barrage in front of the second objective. The completion of the necessary moves will be reported to Divisional Headquarters.

(9) Machine Gun Battalion Headquarters will be located at Advanced Divisional Headquarters - HAGUE FARM.

Right Group Headquarters at Advanced 42nd Infantry Brigade Headquarters H.28.d.

Left Group Headquarters at Advanced 43rd Infantry Brigade Headquarters H.24.c.5.2.

25.9.1918.
S.

Lieut-Col.,
Commanding,
No. 14 Machine Gun Battalion.

Copies to :-

1. Right M.G.Group Comdr.   4. Left M.G.Group Comdr. 4.
2. 34th M.G.Battalion.   5. 35th M.G.Battalion. 5.
3. O.C."B" Company.101st M.G.Bn. 12 C.M.G.O.XIX Corps. 6.
7. War Diary.   File. 8.

SECRET.   Issued with M.G. Instructions No.1.

FIRE ORGANIZATION ORDERS.

Group	Batteries	No. of Guns	Commander	Location of Batteries	Targets	Times. From.	Times. To.	Rate of Fire. R.P.M.	Remarks
RIGHT M.G. GROUP.	"A", "B", "C"	24	Major D. Baxter M.G.	To be selected by Group Commanders & positions notified.	(1) Barrage from 0.2.c.92.62. – 0.3.a.55.75.	H	H + 4	120 per minute.	Groups will be prepared to put down a barrage in front of objective in the event of an I.C.S. between H + 40 and H + 96.
					(2) Lift to line 0.8.d.35.20. – 0.3.b.12.40.	H + 4	H + 13	"	
					(3) Lift to line 0.8.b.74.80. – 0.3.b.57.01.	H + 13	H + 22	"	
					(4) Lift to line 0.9.a.10.37. – 0.3.d.93.57.	H + 22	H + 31	"	
					(5) Lift to line 0.9.c.50.97. – 0.4.c.35.25.	H + 31	H + 40	"	
					(6) Repeat Barrage (5).	H + 96	H + 100	"	

P.T.O.

-2-

LEFT M.G.GROUP.

Group.	Batteries.	No. of Guns.	Commander.	Location of Batteries.	Targets.	Times. From.	Times. To.	Rate of Fire. R.P.M.	Remarks.
	"D", "E", "F"	24	Major C.G.Stephens M.C.	To be selected by Group commander and positions notified.	(1) Barrage 0.3.a.55.75. - 1.34.a.24.36.	H	H + 4	120 per minute.	Groups will be prepared to put down a Barrage before the first objective in the event of an S.O.S. between H.+ 40 and H + 96.
					(2) Lift to line 0.3.b.12.40. - 1.34.c.67.95.	H + 4	H + 13	"	
					(3) Lift to line 0.3.b.57.01. - 1.34.d.20.60.	H + 13	H + 22	"	
					(4) Lift to line 0.3.d.93.67. - 1.34.d.54.25.	H + 22	H + 31	"	
					(5) Lift to line 0.4.c.35.25. - 0.4.b.96.86.	H + 31	H + 40	"	
					(6) Concentrate "F" Battery and Northern half of "E" Battery (12Guns) on Area 0.4.c.75.35. - 0.4.d.10.81.- 0.4.d.65.45. - 0.10.b.26.94.	H + 96.	H + 106.	"	
					(7) "D" Battery & Southern half of "E" Battery repeat Barrage 6.	H + 96.	H + 100.	"	

N.D.

SECRET

14 M.G. BATTN
OPERATION ORDER No. 20

(1) 43rd Inf Bde is advancing to the line of BOUSBUQUE-LINSELLES Rd from BOUSBUQUE inclusive to LINSELLES exclusive. This movement to be completed by 19.00 17th inst. 42nd Inf Bde is not taking part in this advance. 31st Div are occupying LINSELLE.

(2) On completion of this operation 43rd Inf Bde will be holding the whole of the Divisional front.

(3) M.G. Dispositions will be as follows.

(a) A & D Coys distributed in depth will cover the whole Divisional front. Dividing line between Coys will be the line LA RICHE VINAGE W.11 Cent. ROAD JUNCTION W.9 b 5 5. LA MONTAGNE O.C. Coy will report dispositions direct to Batt HQ & 43rd Inf Bde HQ.

(b) B & C Coys will be in Divisional reserve. C Coy will remain at its present location. B Coy to move in the neighbourhood of VAUXHALL FARM starting at 2 p.m.

(4) 43rd Inf Bde HQ is at P.20 d 5.4

(5) Coys to acknowledge by wire.

17/10/18 Copies to
14 Div G   O.C. C Coy
42nd I Bde   O.C. D Coy
43rd I "   Q.M.
O.C. A Coy   War Diary
O.C. B Coy   File

M. Kenny Captain
for Lt Col
14 M.G. BATTN

SECRET.   Copy No. _____

14th MACHINE GUN BATTALION
ORDER NO. 21.

Reference Map 9800.

(1) In confirmation of the warning order No. 132/25 of 26.10.18 the relief therein detailed will take place on the 27/28th October. Relief to be complete by 03.00 on 28th October.

(2) Arrangements for relief will be made direct between Company Commanders concerned.

(3) On completion of the relief the Divisional Boundary will be as follows :-

    Northern.   V.19.c.0.0. thence westward along Grid to GRAND ESPIERRES River, thence along GRAND ESPIERRES River as before.

    Southern.   ESPIERRES CANAL inclusive to B.17.d.3.0. thence westwards along Grid as before.

    Northern Patrol Boundary.   V.19.c.0.0. - V.26.Central.

    Southern Patrol Boundary.   Will be notified later.

    Inter-Company Boundary.   Cross Roads C.4.b.2.9. inclusive to "C" Company, thence in a straight line to Forked Roads U.26.c.9.1. inclusive to "C" Company.

In the event of these alterations in Boundaries altering arrangements already made by Companies, the arrangements made by Companies will stand good, minor adjustments being made after relief.

(4) Headquarters 30th Machine Gun Battalion is at T.18.c.9.4.
    Headquarters "A" Company 30th Machine Gun Battalion at COYGHEM.

(5) Completion of relief will be reported to Battalion Headquarters.

(6) Please acknowledge.

27.10.1918.
S.

Lieut-Col.,
Commanding,
No. 14 Machine Gun Batt'n.

Copies to :-
1. 14th Div."Q"
2. 14th Div."G"
3. 41st Inf.Bde.
4. 42nd Inf.Bde.
5. 43rd Inf.Bde.
6. "A" Company.
7. "B" Company.
8. "C" Company.
9. "D" Company.
10. 30th M.G.Bn.
11. 40th M.G.Bn.
12. Signals.
13. Quartermaster.
14. Medical Officer.
15. B.T.O.
16. Chaplain.
17. War Diary.
18. " "
19. File.

Original "14 M G Bn" Vol 6

Army Form C. 2118.

WAR DIARY
INTELLIGENCE SUMMARY

(Erase heading not required.)

Instructions regarding War Diaries and Intelligence Summaries are contained in F. S. Regs., Part II. and the Staff Manual respectively. Title pages will be prepared in manuscript.

Place	Date	Hour	Summary of Events and Information	Remarks and references to Appendices
NAPIER COPSE.	1.10.1918.		Battalion moved to WYTSCHAETE Area.	14.
	2.10.18.		Battalion moved to LINDENHOEK and then to NEUVE EGLISE on the 3rd instant, with two Companies ("B" & "D") in the Line on the MESSINES - COMINES Front. Locations Battalion Headquarters T.15.b.4.8. "B" Company 0.36.c.95.60. "D" Company P.31.a.85.55. (Map Reference Sheet 28).	
NEUVE EGLISE.	3.10.1918.		The following Officers reported and were posted to Companies :- 2/Lieut. H.Holdstock ("A" Coy.), 2/Lieut. H.D.Weatherhead ("D" Coy.), Lieut. E.C. Catterall ("C" Coy.) Lieut. W.A.Yearwood returned from Hospital and was taken on strength of "B" Company as Transport Officer, Lieut. J.S.Paton being posted to "A" Company vice/C.C.Orrett (killed in action).	
NEUVE EGLISE.	4.10.1918.		"C" Company proceeded to make a Support Line at MESSINES RIDGE. Company Headquarters located at 0.28.d.2.2. (Sheet 28).	
"	5.10.1918.		Night of 5/6th "B" Company relieved Guns of 30th Machine Gun Battalion in Sector YPRES-COMINES CANAL.	15.
"	6.10.1918.		Situation normal. Casualties 1 killed in action, 1 Wounded. Major J.E.Adamson D.S.O. reported from U.K. and assumed Command of "B" Company vice Captain D.Cayley posted to "D" Company who assumed command of that Company from Captain R.Jeffrey.	
"	7.10.1918.		Situation normal.	
"	8.10.1918.		" " "	
"	9.10.1918.		" " " 1 Other Rank wounded. 2/Lieut. Gowans A.C. reported and was posted to "B" Company.	
"	10.10.18.		Conditions normal. 3 casualties (1 wounded, 2 shell shock) during the night "C" Company relieved "D" Company in the Right Sector "D" Company coming into Support.	16.

Army Form C. 2118.

WAR DIARY
or
INTELLIGENCE SUMMARY.
(Erase heading not required.)

Instructions regarding War Diaries and Intelligence Summaries are contained in F. S. Regs., Part II. and the Staff Manual respectively. Title pages will be prepared in manuscript.

Place	Date	Hour	Summary of Events and Information	Remarks and references to Appendices
NEUVE EGLISE.	11.10.18.		Conditions normal. 2 casualties (wounded) during night "A" Company on the Left Sector. "B" Company coming to reserve. 2/Lieut. A.C.Gowans admitted to Hospital.	16.
"	12.10.18.		Conditions normal. (2 casualties wounded).	
"	13.10.18.		Conditions normal. Casualties 2/Lieut. J.A.Broumley slightly wounded and remained at duty. 2 Other Ranks wounded.	
"	14.10.18.		At 05.35 a general attack was made by the Second Army in conjunction with the French and Belgian Armies. The Battalion co-operated with this attack as follows :- "A" Company assisted the operations of the 30th Division by firing a continuous Barrage from 05.35 to 07.5 on the bridges over the River LYS between WERVICQ and WERVICQ SUD. This Barrage was reported to be most effective. Whilst these operations were in progress the 14th Division had to be prepared to force the crossings of the LYS at and on each side of COMINES in the event of the enemy showing signs of relinquishing his positions as a result of the operations further North. In order to be prepared to assist in covering the crossing of the River, a Section each of "A" and "C" Companies were pushed forward to positions from which they could assist the crossings with direct fire, these positions were taken up during the night 13/14th October. All guns were in position by 05.35, 14th October. In addition Companies were prepared to act as laid down in para. 5 of Operation Order No. 17. The 29th Durham Light Infantry succeeded in establishing a small bridgehead immediately North of COMINES during the afternoon, but this was not sufficiently developed for guns to cross. Captain R.Jeffrey proceeded to United Kingdom for duty at Grantham. Authority :- G.H.Q. No. A.G.5631783 (O) dated 9th October, 1918. Casualties 2 Other Ranks wounded, 8 Gassed. Lieut.W.A.Yearwood and Lieut.F.K.Ryder proceeded to United Kingdom for a Tour of Duty. Authority, XV Corps Letter AC.113/8 d/2.10.1918.	17.
"	15.10.18.		The 41st Infantry Brigade succeeded in crossing the LYS South of COMINES and extending their bridgehead North of the town. One section each of "A" and "C" Companies were pushed across the River by 09.00, there was practically no opposition during the day. COMINES was cleared of the enemy and a line established South of the town.	

Army Form C. 2118.

WAR DIARY
or
INTELLIGENCE SUMMARY.
(Erase heading not required.)

Instructions regarding War Diaries and Intelligence Summaries are contained in F. S. Regs., Part II. and the Staff Manual respectively. Title pages will be prepared in manuscript.

Place	Date	Hour	Summary of Events and Information	Remarks and references to Appendices
NEUVE EGLISE.	15.10.18.		Casualties 1 Other Rank (wounded.)	
"	15/16th.		"D" Company with 43rd Infantry Brigade relieved Right Brigade of 30th Division during Night. "B" Company relieved "D" Company in Support on MESSINES RIDGE. Casualties on this day 1 Other Rank.	18.
"	16th to 21st.		43rd Infantry Brigade took over the whole Divisional Front. "A" and "D" Companies acted under Command of B.G.C., 43rd Infantry Brigade during the operations 16th to 21st October (advance from the LYS to the ESCAUT). One Company working with each Battalion in the front line, there was practically no opposition during the advance. Officers Commanding Companies worked in close liason with the Battalion Commanders of the Battalions they were supporting, assisting the advance of the Infantry by engaging hostile Machine Guns and centres of resistance with close range covering fire. The guns were moved almost entirely on their Limbers which were able to move close up to the Infantry Advanced Guard. Company Transport was entirely at the disposal of Officers Commanding Companies during this period.	
"	16.10.18.		Battalion Headquarters with Transport of "A" and "C" Companies moved to Area of VAUXHALL FARM (Sheet 28 P.32.b.) Casualties from forward Companies, 1 Other Rank (Gassed) 3 Other Ranks (wounded)	19.
VAUXHALL FARM.	17.10.18.		43rd Infantry Brigade advanced the Line in accordance with orders attached. "A" and "D" Companies were disposed on the whole Divisional Front in depth, "B" & "C" being in Reserve. "B" Company moved to VAUXHALL FARM, "C" Company remaining at MAXWELL PARK Sheet 28 V.b.2.4. Casualties Lieut. W.H.Cain (N.Y.D.Gas.)	20.
RONCQ.	18.10.18.		Battalion Headquarters and "B" & "C" Companies moved to RONCQ.	
"	19.10.18.		Situation Normal.	
MOUSCRON.	20.10.18.		Battalion Headquarters moved to MOUSCRON. "B" Company to MALGENSE. "C" Company to EVRIGNIES.	

Army Form C. 2118.

WAR DIARY
or
INTELLIGENCE SUMMARY.
(Erase heading not required.)

Instructions regarding War Diaries and Intelligence Summaries are contained in F. S. Regs., Part II. and the Staff Manual respectively. Title pages will be prepared in manuscript.

Place	Date	Hour	Summary of Events and Information	Remarks and references to Appendices
MOUSCRON.	Night 21/22nd.		"B" Company relieved "A" Company. "C" Company relieved "D" Company in the Line.	
	22.10.18.		1 Other Rank Killed in Action.	
LUINGNE.	23.10.18.		Battalion Headquarters moved to LUINGNE Sheet 29(S.23.b.2.0.) 2/Lieut.G.Handley reported and posted to "D" Company. Lieut.W.C.Massey & 2/Lt.A.Rees admitted to Hospital.	
"	24.10.18.		2/Lieut. E.Cartwright reported and posted to "A" Company. 1 Other Rank (G.S.W.)	
"	25.10.18.		Situation normal.	
"	26.10.18.		3 Other Ranks wounded. Lieut. G.R.Macdonald admitted to Hospital.	
"	27.10.18. 27/28th.		2/Lieut. J.Brighton admitted to Hospital. During night of 27/28th a re-adjustment of the Line took place. Part of the 30th Divisional Front being taken over. "B" and "C"Company's Headquarters moved to :- "B" Company. Sheet 37 (C.2.d.80.25.) "C" Company. Sheet 29 (U.20.d. TROIS FARM.	
"	28/29th.		A local operation to obtain possession of the Island at Sheet 37 (E.10.a.) and to force a bridgehead over the River by the 42nd Infantry Brigade assisted by Artillery and "B" and "C" Companies took place at 22.00 and was entirely successful. "C" Company fired 7,500 rounds with 6 guns at known targets in C.11.b and c and "B" Company fired 15,000 rounds with 10 guns at targets in C.6.a. to C.15.d. materially assisting the operation.	
"	29.10.18.		Companies warned to reconnoitre Battery Positions in the event of an advance across the ESCAUT River, also to arrange Forward Dumps in Company Sectors. Casualties 1 Officer (Lieut. S.Black gassed.)	
"	30.10.18.		Harrassing Fire carried out by "B" Company at 22.00 on suspected enemy Machine Gun Positions. 6,000 rounds expended. (Casualty 1 Other Rank wounded.)	
"	31.10.18.		Companies warned that preparations were being made for a crossing of the ESCAUT at HELCHIN and a subsidiary operation East of ESPIERRES.	

signature Lieut. Col.
Commanding 14th Service Battn.,
Machine Gun Corps.

S E C R E T.　　　　　　　　　　　　　　　　　　　　　　　Copy No.

MACHINE GUN BATTALION
ORDER NO. 14.

(1)　　The Battalion will move to WYTSCHAETE Area in accordance with the March Table on reverse.

(2)　　A C K N O W L E D G E.

1st Oct. 1918.　　　　　　　　　　　　　　　(Signed.) W.F. LENNOY, Captain,
S.　　　　　　　　　　　　　　　　　　　　　Adjutant, No. 14 Machine Gun Battalion.

Copies to :-
1. 14th Div. "Q".
2. 14th Div. "G".
3. 41st Inf. Bde.
4. 42nd Inf. Bde.
5. 43rd Inf. Bde.
6. "A" Company.
7. "B" Company.
8. "C" Company.
9. "D" Company.
10. Signals.
11. Quartermaster.
12. Medical Officer.
13. Battn Transport Officer.
14. Padre.
15.)
16.) War Diary.
17. File.

SECRET.

MARCH TABLE TO ACCOMPANY M.G. BATTALION ORDER NO. 14.

Serial No.	Company.	Starting Point	Time.	Route.	Remarks.
1.	Headquarters	OUDERDOM Cross Roads.	13-15	OUDERDOM - BALLBAST Corner - VIERSTRAAT - WYTSCHAETE to Destination.	100 yards intervals to be maintained between Sections.
2.	"B" Company.	"	13-18.		
3.	"C" Company.	"	13-26.		
4.	"D" Company.	"	13-34.		

SECRET.
                                                               Copy No. _____

14th BATTALION M.G. CORPS

OPERATION ORDER NO. 15.

(1)   The 41st Infantry Brigade extended its front to P.30.c.0.3. last night.

   93rd Infantry Brigade took over that portion of the 41st Infantry Brigade Front WEST of the road running through V.1.d.

   The Northern Boundary of the Division is as follows :-

Road Junction P.30.c.0.. (inclusive) to Stream at P.29.b.0.5. westwards along stream to P.21.d.8.0. thence WEST along Grid Line.

(2) (a)   The following Machine Gun Reliefs will take place on the night 5/6th October to be completed by 3 a.m. 6th October.

   "B" Coy. 14th M.G. Battalion will relieve the guns of "B" Coy. 30th Machine Gun Battalion in the Sector YPRES - COMINES Canal (Inclusive) - P.30.c.0.3. (Inclusive), necessary arrangements will be made by Major G.F. Plowden M.C.

   (b)   31st Machine Gun Battalion will relieve the guns of "B" Coy. 14th Machine Gun Battalion in the portion of the front taken over by 93rd Infantry Brigade to-night.

(3) (a)   Headquarters "B" Company, 30th Machine Gun Battalion is near HOUTHEM, P.20.d.1.5.

   (b)   Position of Company of the 31st Machine Gun Battalion will be notified later.

(4)   Completion of relief will be reported to Battalion Headquarters by wiring the Code Word "ISSUED".

                                                    H.G. Lennox
                                                               Captain,
                          Adjutant, No. 14 Machine Gun Battalion.

5.10.1918.
S.

Copies to :-
1. 14th Div. "G".
2. 30th Division.
3. 31st Division.
4. 30th M.G. Battalion.
5. 31st M.G. Battalion.
6. Adv. Battn H.Qrs.
7. 93rd Infantry Bde.
8. 41st Infantry Bde.
9. Medical Officer.
10. O.C. "A" Company.
11. O.C. "B" Company.
12. O.C. "C" Company.
13. O.C. "D" Company.
14. Quartermaster.
15. Signals.
16.) War Diary.
17.)
18. File.

SECRET.   Copy No. X

No. 14 BATTN MACHINE GUN CORPS

ORDER NO. 16.

Reference Sheet 28.

(1)   "C" Company will relieve "D" Company on the right of the Divisional Sector on the night of the 10/11th October, 1918.

"A" Company will relieve "B" Company on the left of the Divisional Sector on the night of the 11/12th October, 1918.

On conclusion of relief :-

"D" Company will be in "Support".
"B" Company in "Reserve".

(2) All Maps, Plans, Trench Stores etc., will be carefully handed and taken over, and receipts obtained. These receipts will be forwarded to the Quartermaster.

(3) All permanent Working Parties and guards will be carefully taken over by the relieving Company in each case.

(4) All information regarding the enemy and details of work in hand and proposed will be taken over by Companies on relief.

(5) All other details of relief will be arranged direct between Officers Commanding Companies concerned.

(6) Completion of relief will be reported to Battalion Headquarters by telegraph, Code Word "CONNECT".

(7) Companies to acknowledge.

9.10.1918.   (Signed.) W.F. LENNOX, Captain,
S.   Adjutant, No. 14 Machine Gun Batt'n.

Copies to :-

1. 14th Div. "G".
2. 41st Inf. Bde.
3. Adv. Headquarters.
4. "A" Company.
5. "B" Company.
6. "C" Company.
7. "D" Company.
8. Signals.
9. Medical Officer.
10. Quartermaster.
11. Battn Transport Officer.
12.)
13.) War Diary.
14. File.

SECRET.   Copy No. 14

14th BATTN MACHINE GUN CORPS
ORDER NO. 17.

Reference Sheet 28 1/40,000.

(1) The 36th British Division are to attack the hostile positions on the point CRUCIFIX FARM (P.30.b.) to KLIETMOLEN (Q.8.c.) at 'H' hour on "J" Day.

The objective of this attack is the approximate line - Railway in P.30.c & b - Q.25.a. - REIKE Village (Incl) - Road Junction Q.17.d.1.1.

The 30th Division are exploiting the success by pushing out Patrols to occupy and to hold WERVICQ and the Line of the LYS in P.36., Q.31., and Q.26.
'H' hour and "J" Day will be notified later.

(2) The attack is being covered by a Field and Heavy Artillery Barrage which will commence at 'H' - 2 minutes, the first lift being timed for 'H' hour.

(3) "A" Company, 14th Machine Gun Battalion will co-operate in this attack by keeping the bridges between WERVICQ and WERVICQ SUD in Q.26.c. under the constant fire of at least one section from 'H' to 'H' plus 2 hours at a rate of 75 rounds per gun per minute.

(4) The following action is being taken in case the pressure of the attack induces the enemy to relinquish his positions on the front of the 14th Division.

(a) The Brigade in the line will be prepared to push Patrols across the River LYS supporting them by stronger bodies and eventually continuing the advance which will be supported by the remainder of the Division.

(b) The direction of the advance to be made will be across the River LYS and then Eastwards towards the line of the high ground in W.2 & 8.

(5) In order to support the advance mentioned in para. (4)

(a) "A" and "C" Companies will each hold one Section in readiness to move forward in immediate support of the Infantry. The guns and ammunition of these sections will be man-handled.

(b) One Section each of "A" and "C" Companies will be prepared to move forward on Pack. As soon as definite orders are given for an advance Pack Animals for these Sections will be sent forward to Company Headquarters of Companies in the line, the orders for these Pack Animals to go up will be issued by Battalion Headquarters. Companies will arrange for the necessary guides to lead them to their destination.

(c) No teams of Pack Animals will be brought forward East of NORTH MIDLAND FARM (T.6.c.) pending definite orders for an advance.

(d) The support and Reserve Companies and remaining Transport of Companies in the line will be prepared to move at ½ an hour's notice after 'H' Hour.   *half*

P.T.O.

-2-

(5) Continued.

(c) Major C.F.Plowden M.C. will arrange with 41st Infantry Brigade as to the action of the Sections mentioned in sub-paras (a) and (b).

(6) In the event of an advance Battalion Headquarters will be established at the present Headquarters of the Support Company. 28/0.26;d.05.40.

(7) Companies and Major C.F.Plowden M.C. to acknowledge.

13.10.1918.

Lieut-Col.,
Commanding,
No. 14 Machine Gun Batt'n.

Copies to :-

1. 14th Div. "G".
2. 41st Inf. Bde.
3. "A" Company.
4. "B" Company.
5. "C" Company.
6. "D" Company.
7. Adv.Battn.Headquarters.
8. Battn Transport Officer.
9. Medical Officer.
10. Quartermaster.
11. Signals.
12.)
13.) War Diary.
14. File.
15. 42nd Inf. Bde.
16. 43rd Inf. Bde.
17. 30th M.G.Batt'n.
18. 31st M.G.Batt'n.

SECRET.

14th BATN. MACHINE GUN CORPS.

Reference para. 3 Order No. 17.

Location of Bridge should read G.15.d.9.2. and not as stated therein.

13.10.1918.
S.

Lieut-Col.,
Commanding,
No. 14 Machine Gun Batt'n.

Copies to all recipients of Order No. 17.

SECRET.   Copy No. X

14th BATTN MACHINE GUN CORPS

ORDER NO. 18.

Reference 28 S.W. & S.E. 1/20,000.

(1) The 43rd Infantry Brigade, 14th Division will relieve the right Brigade of the 30th Division on the 15/16th October, relief to be complete by 06.00 on 16th October. On completion of relief the Eastern and North Eastern Boundary of the Division will be the BLOKSTRAAT CABARET - DUC DE BOURGOGNE CABARET - Road exclusive. The boundary between this point and the LYS will be notified later.

(2) The Machine Gun Defence of the Sector will be taken over by "D" Company - details of relief to be arranged direct between Officer Commanding "D" Company and the Right Group Commander, 30th Machine Gun Battalion whose Headquarters are at Brigade Headquarters P.20.d.5.3.

(3) The approximate positions of the Sections to be relieved are at present

One Section	CRUCIFIX FARM.
One Section	P.24.a. & b.
One Section	S.E.Corner P.18.d.
One Section	Q.13.d.

30th Machine Gun Battalion are retaining the responsibility for the Machine Gun Defence of REEKE HILL Q.20.a & c for the night 15/16th October. "D" Company will take over the defence of the portion of this Hill within the Divisional Boundary on the night 16/17 October. Should the situation have changed between the hour of receipt of this Order and the making of arrangements for the relief by the Company Commanders concerned, O.C. "D" Company will make the necessary dispositions for the Defence of the Sector and report the action taken to Battalion Headquarters.

(4) "B" Company will relieve "D" Company on the MESSINES RIDGE on the 15th October, details to be arranged between Officers Commanding Companies. "B" Company will arrange to send on the necessary Advance Parties to take over accommodation. "D" Company need not await the arrival of "B" Company before moving in relief of the Company, 30th Machine Gun Battalion.

(5) Instructions as to Transport Lines, disposal of Tents, etc., will be notified later.

(6) Please ACKNOWLEDGE.

Issued at
14.10.1918.
S.

Lieut-Col.,
Commanding,
No. 14 Machine Gun Batt'n.

Copies to :-
1. 14th Div. "G".
2. 14th Div. "Q".
3. 41st Inf. Bde.
4. 42nd Inf. Bde.
5. 43rd Inf. Bde.
6. "A" Company.
7. "B" Company.
8. "C" Company.
9. "D" Company.
10. 30th M.G.Batt'n.
11. 30st M.G.Batt'n.
12. Major G.F.Plowden M.C.
13. Signals.
14. Quartermaster.
15. War Diary.
16. "   "
17. File.

SECRET

14 M.G. BATTN.
OPERATION ORDER No 19

Following moves will take place to-day 16th Oct 1918

(1) Batt. H.Q. will move to VAUXHALL FARM P.52.b opening at 2.30 p.m.

(2) Transport A & C Coys will move to area COWES FARM CRISPIN HOUSES or any suitable position in squares P.25 P.26 Starting 3 p.m. if not ordered by their coys to move before.

(3) Transport B Coy to move to vicinity of Coy H.Q. under orders to be issued by O.C. B Coy.

(4) All locations & completion of moves to be notified to Batt. H.Q. as soon as known.

(5) All surplus tents to be collected struck & handed in to QM. All surplus stores to be left at QM. Stores under a guard.

16/10/18

H. Lennox Captain
for Lt. Col.
Commanding 14 M.G. Batt.

Copies to
O.C.
   A Coy
   B "
   C "
   D "
Q.M.
B.T.O.
All Transport Officers
PAG1 Adv.
31st M.G. Battn
30th "
14 Div Q
    G
14 Div Train
S.S.O.

Original

14 Bn. M.G. Corps

Army Form C. 2118.

WAR DIARY
or
INTELLIGENCE SUMMARY.
(Erase heading not required.)

Instructions regarding War Diaries and Intelligence Summaries are contained in F.S. Regs., Part II. and the Staff Manual respectively. Title pages will be prepared in manuscript.

Place	Date	Hour	Summary of Events and Information	Remarks and references to Appendices
LUINGNE.	1.11.1918.		Reliefs of the Companies in the line took place during the night. "A" Company relieved "B" Company. "D" Company relieved "C" Company.	
			Locations of Company Headquarters on completion of reliefs were :-	
			"A" Company. 37/C.2.d.80.25. "C" Company. 29/T.29.d.40.30.	
			"B" Company. 37/B.15.a.99.70. "D" Company. 29/U.20.d. (TROIS FARM).	
			An extension of the line on the left of front took place. Extended to 29/U.24.b.5.5. Casualties 2 Other Ranks (Wounded "B" Company.)	A & B.
"	2.11.1918.		Situation Normal.	
HERSEAUX.	3.11.1918.		Battalion Headquarters moved to HERSEAUX 37/A.5.c.90.30.	
"	4.11.1918.		Harrassing Fire carried out during night of 3/4th. Targets :- Roads in Sheet 37/C.12.c & d. 2,500 rounds fired. 1 Other Rank wounded.	
"	4th/5th.		23,000 Rounds fired to assist 41st Infantry Brigade in throwing 3 bridges in U.30. and U.24 across the ESCAUT and establishing posts on the EAST side. The Operation was successful. The Corps Commander and G.O.C. of the Division complimented all concerned. (Copies attached.)	
"	5.11.1918.		Situation Normal. Casualties 2 Killed, 6 Other Ranks wounded.	
"	5th/6th. 6.11.1918.		During the night Harrassing Fire carried out. 4,000 Rounds were expended on selected targets. Military Medal awarded by Corps Commander to 154623 Pte (L/Cpl) F.HULL, & 30833 Private J.BADGER for Devotion to Duty and Gallantry in action on 25.9.1918.	C.
"	"		During the day an Observation Post in the Tower of POTTES CHURCH (Sheet 29/V.30.d.8.0.75 was fired on with Harrassing Fire.	
			Harrassing Fire was also carried out during night on selected targets. 11,000 Rounds fired. At Midnight the Southern Divisional Boundary was extended to C.15.c.7.3. the new front being taken over from 40th Division. (1 Other Rank wounded.)	23.

Army Form C. 2118.

WAR DIARY
or
INTELLIGENCE SUMMARY.
(Erase heading not required.)

Instructions regarding War Diaries and Intelligence Summaries are contained in F. S. Regs., Part II. and the Staff Manual respectively. Title pages will be prepared in manuscript.

Place	Date	Hour	Summary of Events and Information	Remarks and references to Appendices
HERSEAUX.	7.11.1918.		Situation Normal. Church Tower, POTTES was again the subject of our Machine Gun Fire. 350 Rounds expended during the day. Harrassing Fire carried out during the night on selected targets, 3,000 Rounds fired. Part of the Divisional Front in the North was handed over to 30th Division. Northern Boundary then running from U.30.c. Casualties Lieut. O.P.Ladly GSW., 2 Other Ranks (NYD Gas.)	24.
"	8.11.1918.		Quiet day. Instructions sent to Companies to cross the ESCAUT in the event of the enemy retiring. Observation Post in POTTES CHURCH again fired on during the day. Lieut. H.D.Weatherhead admitted to Hospital (Sick).	D.
"	9.11.1918.		Enemy retired, and the crossing of ESCAUT began at once. "A" Company had two sections across by 12.00. These two Sections reached 37/D.25.central and Min Butor 37/D.20.c. respectively. Guns and ammunition were man-handled the whole way. At 11.00 a section of "D" Company crossed the River man-handling the guns and established themselves in LANNOY. At 12.00 1 Section of "D" Company had crossed the River at U.30.central, the men crossing by a floating footbridge and the mules swimming. At 13.00 this Section moved forward to BOIS-CANU in 37/D.14.d.	
"	10.11.1918.		The Final objective having been reached the Battalion was withdrawn from the Line. Companies assembled at DOTTIGNIES with Battalion Headquarters at HERSEAUX.	
"	14.11.1918.		Lieut.S.Black and 2/Lieut.J.Brighton reported from Hospital and were re-taken on strength. 2/Lieuts.A.S.H.Johnson and G.Wilding reported from Base Depot and were posted to "D" Coy. D.C.M. awarded by Field Marshal Commanding-in-Chief to 153848 Private J.S.QUINLAN, "C" Coy.	E.
TOURCOING.	16.11.1918.		Battalion moved to TOURCOING in accordance with attached Order (No. 25). Battalion and Company Headquarters were located as follows :- Battalion Headquarters :- 35, Rue de LILLE. 36/F.4.d.3.4. "A" Company. 14 Rue de SENTIER. 36/F.10.b.1.4. "B" Company. 21. Rue de la Blanche Port. 36/F.10.a.8.3. "C" Company. 220, Rue de Paris. 36/F.9.a.8.3. "D" Company. 1, Bis. Rue Gambetta. 36/F.9.a.8.1. 2/Lieut.James R. reported from Base Depot, & was posted to "A" Company.	25.

A6945 Wt. W14422/M1160 350,000 12/16 D. D. & L. Forms/C/2118/14.

Army Form C. 2118.

WAR DIARY
or
INTELLIGENCE SUMMARY.

(Erase heading not required.)

Instructions regarding War Diaries and Intelligence Summaries are contained in F. S. Regs., Part II. and the Staff Manual respectively. Title pages will be prepared in manuscript.

Place	Date	Hour	Summary of Events and Information	Remarks and references to Appendices
TOURCOING.	20.11.18.		Lieut.H.D.Weatherhead returned from Hospital and was re-taken on strength of "D" Company. Lieut. E.L.Wood proceeded to GRANTHAM for Tour of Duty in United Kingdom, and was struck off strength. (Authority A.G.'s No.5990 (o) dated 7.11.1918.)	
"	28.11.18.		2/Lieut. Lomax J.A. reported from Base Depot, and was posted to "B" Company. 2/Lieut.Smart H.W. proceeded to OXFORD for Educational Course.(Authority 14th Division G.O.149 dated 28.11.1918.)	
"	29.11.18.		Lieut. Iredale E.W. proceeded to United Kingdom for Tour of Duty at GRANTHAM, and was struck off strength. (Authority 14th Division G.S.1520 dated 10.11.1918.)	
"	30.11.18.		The Battalion took part in a parade of the Division for Inspection by the XV Corps Commander.	

1.12.1918.
S.

Lieut-Col.,
Commanding,
14th Batt'n, Machine Gun Corps.

To:- 14th Machine Gun Batt'n.

G.O. 54 5.11.1918. Following from XV Corps begins. Corps Commander congratulates you and all concerned on successfull operations carried out last night. Ends.

                                              14th Division.

14th Division
G.S.1470.

14th Machine Gun Batt'n.

It is with the utmost pride and pleasure that I congratulate the troops of the 14th Division on the highly successful operation carried out last night;

Once more this success was due to the close and cordial co-operation of every arm of the service and I offer my most sincere thanks to the 41st Infantry Brigade and all the troops associated with them.

(Signed.) P.B.SKINNER, Major-General,
Commanding, 14th Division.

5th Novr.1918.

A.S.4/50.

14th Batt'n, M.G. Corps.

    Under authority delegated by the Field Marshal Commanding-in-Chief, the Corps Commander has awarded the following Decorations for gallantry and devotion to duty in action :-

THE MILITARY MEDAL.

No. 154623 Private (Lce.Corpl.) F. HULL   M.G. Corps.
     30833 Private, J. BADGER,   M.G. Corps.

5th November, 1918.

H.M.

(Signed.) P.V. DAVIES, Captain,
for A.A. & Q.M.G.,
14th Division.

SECRET.   Copy No. 11

14th BATTN MACHINE GUN CORPS

ORDER NO. 23.

(1) (a) On the night 6th/7th November, 14th Division will hand over to 30th Division that portion of the Divisional Front North of U.30.c.central.   Relief to be complete by 00.01 November 7th.

   (b) The bridge at U.30.c.central will be inclusive to 14th Division.

(2)   In connection with this relief "D" Company will arrange direct to hand over to the right Machine Gun Company of the 30th Division any gun positions covering the present Divisional Front North of U.30.c.central. The sub-section at U.29.b.0.5. will be retained by "D" Company. Headquarters right Machine Gun Company, 30th Division is at O.35.a.1.2.

(3)   Completion of relief to be reported to Battalion Headquarters and 41st Infantry Brigade.

(4)   "D" Company to acknowledge.

                                              H.Y. Lemay Captain
                                                    /o/
                                                    Lieut-Col.,
                                                    Commanding,
5.11.1918.   14th Batt'n, Machine Gun Co
S.

            Copies to :-
              1. 14th Div."G".
              2. 14th Div."Q".
              3. 41st Inf.Bde.
              4. "A" Company.
              5. "B" Company.
              6. "C" Company.
              7. "D" Company.
              8. 30th M.G.Batt'n.
              9. 39th M.G.Batt'n.
             10. Signals.
             11. War Diary.
             12. "   "
             13. File.

SECRET.   Copy No. 11

14th BATT'N MACHINE GUN CORPS
ORDER NO. 24.

(1) (a) On the night 6th/7th November, 1918, the 14th Division will take over from the 40th Division the front from the present Southern Boundary to C.15.c.7.3.
Relief will be complete by 00.01 November 7th.

(b) In connection with this relief "A" Company will arrange direct to take over from the Left Machine Gun Company of the 40th Division all gun positions covering the new Divisional Front North of C.15.c.7.3.

(c) On completion of relief the Southern Boundary will run from C.15.c.7.3. to Bridge B.18.c.5.9. (inclusive to 14th Division) thence along present boundary.

(d) Completion of relief to be reported to Battalion Headquarters and 41st Infantry Brigade.

(2) (a) Relief as stated in Order No. 23 dated 5.11.1918 will now be carried out on the night 7th/8th November.

(b) On completion of relief the Northern Divisional Boundary will run from U.30.c.5.5. to U.8.b.2.8. thence South West along present Boundary.

(3) "A" and "D" Companies to acknowledge.

                                            Lieut-Col.,
                                            Commanding,
6.11.1918.   14th Batt'n. Machine Gun Corps.
S.

Copies to :-

1. 14th Div."G".
2. 14th Div."Q".
3. 41st Inf.Bde.
4. "A" Company.
5. "B" Company.
6. "C" Company.
7. "D" Company.
8. 30th M.G.Batt'n.
9. 39th M.G.Batt'n.
10. Signals.
11. War Diary.
12. "   "
13. File.

SECRET.

SS.133/1.

To:- Officer Commanding,
"A" Coy.   "C" Coy.
"B" Coy.   "D" Coy.

Reference Sheet 37 1/40,000.

(1) Should the enemy retire before 'J' day, the Division is to cross the ESCAUT and keep touch with him as far as the line Farm in J.1.a. - Farm in D.25.d. - D.26.b.2.8. - Cross Roads in D.20.d.5.9 only.

(2) The Advanced Guard consisting of

      The Infantry Brigade in the Line.
      1 Battery R.F.A. (18 Pdrs.)
      1 Section Howitzers.
      2 Companies M.G.Battalion.
      1 Section, R.E.

will cross the ESCAUT and advance to the line given in para. 1.

(3) (a) Should the advance take place before 18.00 hours on J - 1 day the Companies allotted to the advanced guard will be

      "A" and "D" Companies.

(b) Should the advance take place between 18.01 hours on J - 1 day and "H" hour the Companies allotted to the advanced guard will be

      "B" and "C" Companies.

(c) Companies will be prepared to move 2 sections per Company on pack.

(4) The Officer Commanding Advanced Guard is the B.G.C. the Brigade in the Line.

                                                Lieut-Col.,
                                                Commanding,
                                    14th Batt'n, Machine Gun Corps.

8.11.1918.
S.

Copies to :-   14th Div., "G",
                14th Div. Artillery,
                41st Inf. Bde,
                42nd Inf. Bde,
                43rd Inf. Bde,
                Signals.
                Medical Officer.

Under authority delegated by His Majesty the King, the Field Marshal Commanding-in-Chief has awarded the following Decoration :-

DISTINGUISHED CONDUCT MEDAL.

No. 153848 Pte J.S.Quinlan.   "C" Company.

Throughout the Operations on 28.9.1918 Pte Quinlan led his Team very successfully. When the Infantry were held up he pushed forward and mounted his gun at the final objective from which the enemy had retired. A party of enemy attempted to return but were prevented from doing so by Pte Quinlan's gun, which inflicted heavy casualties.

Later seeing that a party of Infantry were held up by an Officer and two Snipers in a Pill-Box, he and another man returned, and cleared out the Pill-box, killing the three Germans with Revolvers.

His Conduct was a fine example to all.

S E C R E T.
Copy No. 9

14th BATT'N, MACHINE GUN CORPS.
ORDER NO. 25.

(1) The Battalion will move to TOURCOING on November 16th, 1918.

(2) Move will be carried out in accordance with attached March/table.

(3) One Officer and one guide will meet Major G.F.Plowden M.C. at the Area Commandant's Office, TOURCOING at 10.00.

(4) Motor Lorries have been asked for, one to report to "B" Company for use of "B" and "D" Companies.
One to report to "A" Company for use of "A" and "C" Companies.

(5) Blankets and Greatcoats will be carried in the Lorries.
Leather Jerkins and Waterproof sheets will be carried in the Pack.

(6) Battalion Headquarters will close at HERSEAUX at 11.00 and open at TOURCOING at the same hour.

(7) Companies to acknowledge.

(Signed.) W.F. LENNOX, Captain,
Adjutant, No. 14 Machine Gun Battalion.

Copies to :-

1. 14th Div. "G".
2. 14th Div. "Q".
3. "A" Company.
4. "B" Company.
5. "C" Company.
6. "D" Company.
7. Battn Transport Officer.
8. Signals.
9. War Diary.
10. "   "
11. File.

MARCH TABLE TO ACCOMPANY ORDER NO. 25.

Company.	Starting Point.	Time.	Route.	Remarks.
Headquarters.	HERSEAUX.	To be	notified.	(1) Last Company will be clear of Railway Crossing PETIT AUDENARDE by 10.00 hours.
"A" Company.	X Roads at T.5.a.20.50.	08.30.	PETIT AUDENARDE WATERLOS.	
"B" Company.	"	08.35.	"	
"C" Company.	"	08.40.	"	
"D" Company.	"	08.45.	"	

14 Bn M.G. Corps

Army Form C. 2118.

WAR DIARY
or
INTELLIGENCE SUMMARY.
(Erase heading not required.)

Instructions regarding War Diaries and Intelligence Summaries are contained in F. S. Regs., Part II. and the Staff Manual respectively. Title pages will be prepared in manuscript.

Place	Date	Hour	Summary of Events and Information	Remarks and references to Appendices
TOURCOING.	30.11.1918.		Lieut. G.R.Macdonald reported from Hospital and was retaken on strength.	
"	9.12.18.		The Battalion paraded with the 14th Division for Inspection by the XV Corps Commander.	
"	5.12.18.		Croix-de-Guerre - Corps Star awarded to Lieut-Colonel L.R.Meade-Waldo D.S.O. Croix-de-Guerre - Brigade awarded to No. 23796 Pte Yates G.	
"	11.12.19.		Captain A.St.Johnston (R.A.M.C.) was sent for duty with Argyle and Sutherland Highlanders, the medical duties of the Unit being taken over by 44th Field Ambulance.	
			During the month Infantry and Machine Gun training was carried out as well as Educational and Recreational training.	

Lieut.-Col.
Commanding 14th Service Battn.,
Machine Gun Corps.

Army Form C. 2118.

14 Bn M.G Corps

WAR DIARY
or
INTELLIGENCE SUMMARY.
(Erase heading not required.)

Instructions regarding War Diaries and Intelligence Summaries are contained in F.S. Regs., Part II. and the Staff Manual respectively. Title pages will be prepared in manuscript.

Place	Date	Hour	Summary of Events and Information	Remarks and references to Appendices
TOURCOING.	1.1.1919. to 6.1.1919.		Nothing to report.	
"	6.1.1919.		Inspection of Battalion by General Officer Commanding, 14th Division.	
"	7.1.1919.		7850 C.S.M.Sherratt H. and 154534 Cpl Sewart T. awarded Belgian Crois-de-Guerre.	
"	7.1.1919 to 31.1.1919.		Nothing to report.	
"	31.1.1919.		Numbers demobilized from 1st to 31st - 10 Officers, 249 Other Ranks.	
	1.2.1919. S.			

Romun Captain
Lieut-Col.,
Commanding,
14th Batt'n, Machine Gun Corps.

Army Form C. 2118.

WAR DIARY
or
INTELLIGENCE SUMMARY.
(Erase heading not required.)

Instructions regarding War Diaries and Intelligence Summaries are contained in F. S. Regs., Part II. and the Staff Manual respectively. Title pages will be prepared in manuscript.

Vol 10

Place	Date	Hour	Summary of Events and Information	Remarks and references to Appendices
TOURCOING.	1.2.19 to 21.2.19.		Nothing to report.	
"	22.2.19.		Lieut.(A/Major D.Baxter M.C. transferred to Home Establishment.	
"	22.2.19 to 28.2.19.		Nothing to report.	
"	1.2.19 to 28.2.19.		14 Officers and 230 Other Ranks transferred to U.K. for demobilization.	

Tourcoing,
28.2.1919.
S.

[signature]
Lieut-Col.,
Commanding,
14th Batt'n, Machine Gun Corps.

www.ingramcontent.com/pod-product-compliance
Lightning Source LLC
Chambersburg PA
CBHW081445160426
43193CB00013B/2392